D0645309

CROSS FUNCTIONAL INFLUENCE
Getting Things Done Across the Organization

CROSS FUNCTIONAL INFLUENCE
Getting Things Done Across the Organization

by Susan Z. Finerty

Copyright © 2019 by Susan Z. Finerty

All rights reserved. No part of this publication may be reproduced, stored in a retrieval system, or transmitted, in any form or by any means, electronic, mechanical, photocopying, recording, or otherwise, without the prior written permission of the author.

ISBN-13: 978-1-5456-5342-5

LCCN: 2019931692

Printed in the United States of America

To my children, Meg, Abby and Sean:
A reminder that you can do anything you put your mind to.

And to my Dad, Eugene Zelmanski,
who always reminded me of the same thing.

Contents

Acknowledgements

This book was a lot of fun to write, for many reasons. First, because it started with my first book, *Master the Matrix: 7 Essentials for Getting Things Done in Complex Organizations*, then grew through the sessions and discussions with participants in my course at the University of Wisconsin-Madison. It has been so satisfying to see it blossom and then captured on these pages. So to Steve King, Chuck West and Karen Kulcinski at UW, thank you for giving me the opportunity and for all your support!

Second, it was a lot of fun because it allowed me time with some of the most delightful and capable people I know!

Once again, my editor, Emilie Croisier, hit the ball out of the park. This book was presented to her in a much more "raw" state than the last one, and she was able to smooth it out when I could not! Emilie makes me sound smart, and my designer, Kevin Fitzgerald, makes it look beautiful. Kevin took ugly Word documents with mismatched fonts, handwritten notes and scraps of emails, and turned it all into a gorgeous product. Wally Bock, my writing coach, was once again simultaneously brutally honest and hopelessly optimistic about this project from start to finish.

And to my family and friends who patiently listened through my ideas and cheered me on—thank you, for seeing me through this project and so many others! Last, but certainly not least, to my kids, Meg, Abby and Sean. I know I try not to have my writing get in the way of being your mom—but it does. In the end, I hope it is worth it—to experience someone living out their dream and accomplishing their goals. All three of you have the same light in you—burn on!

The average of responses to the question:

"What percentage of your job do you get done through your formal authority?"

asked in Cross-Functional Influence Workshops.

Introduction

Influence Is How Things Get Done

Mike, *an emergency room doctor, had just made the move from clinical practice to a role in administration, leading the efforts to introduce new information technology to the hospital system, when the need for influence hit him and hit him hard.*

"I had what I thought was a title and credentials that could make things happen—I assumed the title and the letters after my name said it all. When I started, I knew I needed to make some big changes. That's essentially why they brought me in. I did a great job asking questions—I asked a ton of them. So I didn't fall into the 'know-it-all' trap. The mistake I made was that once I asked the questions, I just declared what I wanted done. I'd send an email, maybe call a meeting and tell people.

"What I didn't realize was that this approach (some labeled it 'Mike's Proclamations,' others called it strong-arming, although I didn't know that at the time) was all wrong. I was relying on my title's 'power' and doing nothing to build ownership or understanding or real sustainable change. I was treating everyone as if it was the ER and they all worked for me, and telling them what I wanted. No collaboration, no working together—just declarations, based on my own opinions and needs. No real influence.

"So I got the feedback, and I started pulling people in. I finally saw that when working cross-functionally, I had to do things differently. But then something really blew me away. My boss pulled me aside and said the declarations weren't working for my team, either. They needed to be influenced, and I needed to collaborate more with them to establish a sense of ownership in the changes.

"And then he said something that will always stick with me: 'Mike, anybody can play the title card—that doesn't take much skill or finesse. Real influence comes from building relationships, ownership and getting people engaged. Even the CEO has to influence—title just doesn't matter.'"

Stephanie was in a different situation. She was a project manager with more responsibility than could fit in a job description and formal authority of exactly zero. She didn't have the title, she didn't have authority—but what she did have were some enormous milestones for a pharmaceutical product in her company's development pipeline.

People thought she was crazy to take the job. In fact, the project had already spit out three other managers who either tired of not making progress or burned bridges so badly in their attempt to make progress that the organization rejected them.

She could have lobbied for resource authority—some direct reporting relationships to the project team. She could have made a case for a bigger title. Instead she focused on relationships—both on and outside the team. She deliberately reached out to people to build trust, get input and build buy-in. She got to know the business and business needs as well as the informal workings and the "chess game" required to get things done. She

© 2019 ◯FINERTY CONSULTING

realized a crucial part of the game was thinking several steps ahead and anticipating the reactions of others. And she communicated, dialogued and persevered through a lot of information gathering, consensus building and difficult conversations that others simply weren't willing to do.

Mike and Stephanie's stories will unfold throughout this book. Mike provides great illustrations of the pitfalls, and through Stephanie's story you will see what it looks like when it's done right—how she used the energy that others exerted trying to fight the model to make the model work for her.

What ever happened to authority?

Mike and Stephanie represent a common reality in today's organizations—formal authority (represented on org charts and in titles) simply isn't the driver it once was. Cross-functional teams, project teams, center-led functions, centers of excellence, shared services and "flatter" organizations have blurred and in some cases completely erased traditional lines of authority. Gone are the days when your title defined your power and decision-making rights. Today, influence reigns as both king and queen of our organizations.

The influence we are talking about here is not your traditional persuasion. It's not the used car salesman urging you to buy the "real gem" of a beat-up Chevy. It's not easy. Influencing takes strategy, planning, and plenty of patience and perseverance.

The problems we face, decisions we make and projects we run are complex—a reflection of the sophisticated products our organizations design and manufacture, markets they operate in, and regulatory environments they must navigate. Very rarely does all this work reside neatly in one function, team or location—our work and our organizations have become *cross-functional*. It requires us to reach across functions and geographical boundaries. And once that reach happens, influence is required—because unless you have the biggest title on the organizational chart, your authority doesn't cover it all. And where authority ends, influence begins.

Now here's where things get really tricky: when you are influencing across the organization, goals, priorities, objectives and agendas often conflict. It's one thing to convince a fellow IT person of the value of a common technology platform. Try getting HR to buy into the same technology platform as Finance. Or any common platform at all—even the idea of a platform! Influence replaces authority with a twist: not only do you not have the leverage that authority provides, you must collaborate with people who see the organization from a completely different perspective.

Influence Ingredients: Proactive and In the Moment

There are two types of people who can influence—those who are persuasive conversationalists and those who build up influence equity over time. Not surprisingly, the latter are the ones who can have a sustained effect in organizations.

When you are influencing cross-functionally, relationships are key. I call these relationships "partnerships" (more on this in Section 1). In cross-functional work, you are either influencing a current partner (and through this influence opportunity have a chance to develop the partnership or leverage the current state of the partnership) or you are influencing someone who may well become a partner in the future. Influence in organizations rarely happens in isolation—it usually won't be your first or last interaction with the person you are trying to influence. What that means is that your level of influence starts well before you jot a few persuasive ideas down on paper or put together a couple of compelling PowerPoint slides—it's built over months and years and is all about your credibility and reputation in the organization. It also means that how you handle the opportunity to influence impacts not only the issue at hand but also your partnership and future influence prospects.

I introduced five influence ingredients in *Master the Matrix*. Here, I've expanded that list to six and built a new model to describe them.

© 2019 ○FINERTY CONSULTING

Three ingredients are developed over time, *proactively*. The other three are situational, opportunity-based and applied *in the moment*:

You reap what you sow when influencing in your organization. The "sowing" is what I call the "**Proactive**" ingredients. These include forging partnerships in your organization (*Section 1*), building trust by demonstrating willingness to be influenced (*Section 2*) and building knowledge of the organization (*Section 3*). This sowing takes place all the time. Each day is an opportunity to build trust, credibility and equity in the organization, which can all be applied when it comes to the moment of truth—actually influencing something.

The **"In the Moment"** ingredients are those you apply to a specific influence opportunity. They include *prepare*—identifying and assessing the people you will be influencing and framing your message (*Section 4*), *dialogue*—how you conduct a conversation that lends itself to influence (*Section 5*) and *follow-up*—making sure that what you have influenced actually gets implemented (*Section 6*).

We will look at each of these ingredients in the sections that follow, but know that for any given situation, you may not need all six. Establish the three proactive ingredients, and the in-the-moment ingredients don't have to be 100% buttoned-down. If you don't have the proactive ingredients in place, you will have to really excel in the moment—when trust is not established, a highly effective dialogue is needed to fill the void.

Using this model in the sections that follow, I take the approach of slowing things way down—really thinking through and planning the process of influencing. Think of it like learning a physical skill, for example hitting a golf ball. The golf pro will have you slow down your swing (either literally or on video) to analyze it and make improvements. That's what I will be doing with influence. In the end, these techniques can be applied both in a planned way well ahead of time and spontaneously when someone stops you in the hall with something you need to influence on the spot.

Getting the most out of this book

I want this book to be a resource that you turn to over and over again, that you bookmark, highlight and cover with Post-it notes (at least for those of you reading the old-fashioned print version).

I would also encourage you to read it with a couple past and future influence opportunities in mind. There are hundreds of practical tips throughout the book that really shine when you put them in the context of your own influence experiences and goals.

Want to take it further?

If you really want to go in depth to build your skills or the skills of others, check out our *Cross-Functional Influence Playbook*. This playbook maps to this book and has dozens of assessments, worksheets and planning tools. Also check out the Finerty Consulting website at www.finertyconsulting.com for information on our cross-functional influence workshops and simulations, e-learning and online assessment tools.

© 2019 ◯FINERTY CONSULTING

A final note before you start

As with any resource, the real value of this book is your personal commitment to trying things out and taking a risk. These tips may not work the first time, or you may feel clumsy. And that's hard when you are anxious and ready, maybe even urgently ready, to improve. Give yourself a break—try the ideas a couple of times, with different people, to see what works for you in your organization. Also give others a break—it may take them some time to adjust to your new behaviors!

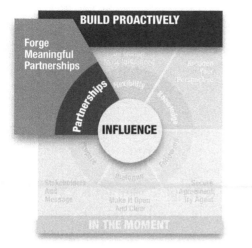

"You cannot antagonize and influence at the same time."

J.S. KNOX

Section 1: Partnerships

In Our Complex Organizations, No Endeavor Is Purely Independent

❝ *Unequivocally, he cannot succeed here.* ❞ These were the words of an executive coach hired to assist Mike, the subject of our opening story. In his first six months, Mike had torn through an IT group and several partner groups around the hospital system, leaving the landscape barren. After bullying, threatening and strong-arming various partners in the organization, his trust was shot. People were now actively rallying against anything he wanted just as a matter of principle. Instead of building partnerships, Mike was building walls that were destroying any chance he had to gain support within the organization. Without partnerships, he couldn't influence. And without influence, anyone who relies heavily on cross-functional buy-in to achieve their goals will quickly find themselves stuck. Mike had dug himself into a very deep hole, one that even the best of executive coaches was struggling to extract him from.

A lot of heavy lifting is necessary to get things done in today's organizations, and partnerships—those relationships/connections that the business creates—lighten the load. Tasks that fall entirely under the control of one person are rare. Whatever your role, you will always be pulling in outside expertise, approval, arms and legs for implementation—absolutely dependent on others to accomplish your goals.

In today's multitasking, geographically dispersed workforce, most partnerships don't just happen. Even when they do, we tend to be too narrow in our field of partners. To be influential in the organization, your field of partners needs to be broad.

The partnerships you need to form may not be convenient or comfortable. In our cross-functional organizations, you will find yourself working with people in different locations, time zones, and with very different experiences and preferences. You don't have proximity and may not have personal chemistry on your side. Talking about good relationships in a negotiating setting, Fisher and Brown wrote in *Getting Together: Building Relationships as We Negotiate* (1989): "While it is easier to build a good road across a prairie than through mountains, a good road through mountains may be more valuable than one across a prairie."

Like a road through a mountain, some partnerships can be difficult to build, but the effort pays off if the destination is of mutual benefit. Without mutual benefit, your attempts to form partnerships can be seen as trying to create pawns or build a network on your way up the corporate ladder. The partnerships we will talk about in this section are sustainable, long-term, mutually beneficial relationships that are built intentionally and in an earnest way.

The critical connection: Partners and Influence

What is the critical connection between partnerships and influence? Why are partnerships the starting point for our model? First, as we just

© 2019 ⭕FINERTY CONSULTING

learned in the opening scenario, where there is trust, there is influence. Simply put, partners require less convincing—think fewer PowerPoint slides! You start off several steps ahead—they trust you, so the background noise is gone, and you are able to focus on the merits of the idea or request versus building your own personal credibility.

But the impact of strong partners goes well beyond the ease you can find in influencing them directly. They can also help you through their own networks. Stephanie, from our opening story, provided a great description on this. "I wanted to convince Mary to allocate a resource from her team to my project. I didn't know Mary, but I knew Ed, who had a really strong partnership with both Mary and me. So although I didn't have a direct line to Mary, my decision-maker, I had an indirect line via Ed. So I asked myself how I could leverage my partnership with Ed to influence Mary? I realized I had a lot of options—he could be a great resource!"

What Stephanie realized was that partners expand your influence in a variety of ways, ranging from providing perspective to actually influencing for you—being your surrogate:

| Perspective | Advocate | Ally | Surrogate |

In Stephanie's example, as Mary's partner, Ed could provide *perspective*. He can share insights on her hot buttons, views and experiences with what Stephanie is proposing, along with suggestions based on how he has seen her be influenced in the past.

Ed could be Stephanie's *advocate*, "Mary, I know that Stephanie has set up time to talk to you this week about securing a resource from your team—she knows her stuff, and it sounds like there might be a good fit there."

Or maybe it makes sense to bring Ed into the conversation—he could be Stephanie's *ally* and participate in the conversation with Mary.

Finally, Ed could be Stephanie's *surrogate*—he could influence Mary for her, on her behalf.

Partners—whether you leverage them for perspective, as an advocate, ally or surrogate, broaden your network of influence in the organization. They are absolutely essential to becoming a real influencer.

Who should your partners be?

"So, Mike, what's the biggest difference between your previous role and this one?" I asked, more as an introductory conversation starter than a formal question to Mike, who had dug a deep hole through his lack of partnerships. Here is his direct quote: "There are a hell of a lot more people to piss off in this role." At that point Mike was off and running. He had spent the better part of his short tenure stepping on landmines and chasing rabbits down holes.

His relationship requirements had gone from fairly simple, one-dimensional connections with the chief of his division and the staff in the ER to a multi-dimensional matrix of potential partners. As with many roles, an endless number of people had to, or wanted to, give input into what he was doing. Mike resented this and reacted by trying to build boundaries. According to Mike, "Consulting with people in every nook and cranny of the hospital system on my project and my responsibilities just slows me down." His approach was not only off-putting to his partners, it was leading him to make decisions that missed the mark. In other words, the "mind your own business" approach was failing miserably.

True organizational influence requires you to look outside of your team, your silo and your immediate geographic area to identify whom you need to work with and through. It is usually well outside the traditional "us." In Mike's case, he defined "us" as the people who shared his expertise; anyone else was "them" and wasn't allowed in.

But Mike didn't stop there. He also lamented about the junior IT folks who were asking him questions and with whom he was supposed to "consult." Frustrated by people below him hounding him, he shut them out. He didn't realize that in order to get things done, he should be building relationships and influencing in all directions. In cross-functional organizations you will find yourself interacting and partnering with people at all levels of the organization—up, down, sideways, diagonal. The projects and issues most of us find ourselves involved in almost always include multiple levels and functions.

So, the lesson of this story—don't make the same mistakes Mike did. Strike the right balance between being too limiting in the parameters of whom you work to partner with (and thereby leaving critical people out) and casting too wide a net (including, to the extreme, making such partnerships superficial and meaningless).

Start by looking at how your role is structured. Every job is divided up differently—yours might be categorized by project, customer or area of responsibility. Then ask yourself about the different people who are involved:

HAND-OFFS	Whom do you work hand in hand with? Whom do you hand things off to? Who hands things off to you?
WHO HAS...	Power to veto your decisions or implementation of decisions? Knowledge, experience or expertise to tap into? Opinion leadership that can sway others you need to influence? Authority over resources needed to make or implement decisions?
WHOM DO YOU NEED TO...	Demonstrate support (in word and deed)? Convince or permit others to support? Add something to their to-do list?

These are basically the people who touch your work. I think of it as a series of adjacencies—to varying degrees these people interact or overlap with your job responsibilities. You can see these touchpoints visually, as well:

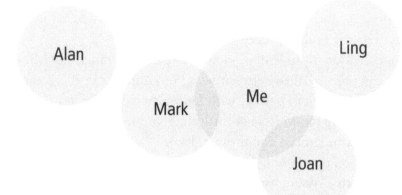

If they touch your circle at all, chances are someday you will need to influence them. And if influence is required, then it must be preceded by partnership and trust.

This list is a snapshot—your partners aren't static. They can change by project, as people move in and out of a team or organization, as project scopes shrink or expand, and as decisions are made. This exercise is not one that you complete and put on the shelf. Influencers are constantly asking themselves whom they should be partnering closely with. You don't need to be attached at the hip with each of these partners—there are gradations of partnerships to consider.

The Matrix–Partner Continuum™

Partnerships can take many different forms ranging from simple hand-offs of information or work products to close integration of tasks and goals. You will have to influence partnerships in all categories.

© 2019 ○FINERTY CONSULTING

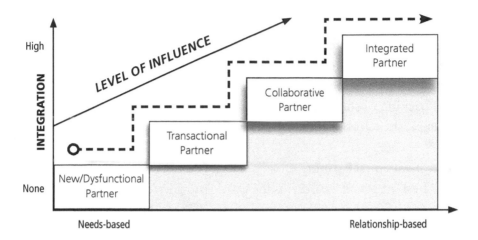

The vertical axis in this chart is the degree to which partners integrate or organize their work around each other—to what extent they align goals, make decisions and plan based on the other's business. Ryan, a global product manager, defined the highest level of partnering as "when you are willing to change the way you do business or change your goals or your direction based on input and expertise from another person."

The needs-to-relationship axis is based on the degree to which the partnership is grounded solely in the business need or extended or enhanced based on the relationship. It is assumed that any partnership includes a business need (otherwise these relationships are at-will friendships), but moving along this continuum depends on extending beyond "I work with you because I need you" to "I work with you because we make each other better at what we do."

Here are the basic definitions of each of these partnerships:

1. New/Dysfunctional Partners

New/Dysfunctional partnerships occur where there is need but no integration. The business has brought people or teams together, but they remain separate in terms of their relationship—either because the partnership is too new or because the partners have fallen into a pattern of competing, comparing or judging each other. The hallmark of dysfunctional partnerships is lack of trust—which strains communication and turns conflict into competition.

What can you influence with this partner? Not much unless you have the backing of some authority (either your own or someone else's). In essence, the relationship and lack of trust will get in the way of influence.

2. Transactional Partners

The Transactional Partner is the classic provider/consumer relationship. The focus is on hand-offs and exchanges. The tasks that connect Transactional Partners are likely process-based, routine and perhaps even repetitive. The keys to success in these partnerships are reliability and consistency (which build trust), keeping partners well informed and addressing conflicts as they arise in a constructive manner. These practices ensure smooth exchanges. A strong transactional partnership is a well-oiled machine.

What can you influence with this partner? Smaller tactical items, like a small shift in priorities, task deadline, etc. Bigger decisions, overall goals and behaviors are going to be tougher at this level.

3. Collaborative Partners

Just to the left of Integrated Partners on the needs-to-relationship axis are Collaborative Partners. Less discrete tasks and closer coordination are the hallmarks of Collaborative Partners. Hand-offs are supplemented with regular communication to confer and debrief. Not only are there many hand-offs, but some tasks are completed hand in hand. Success in these partnerships is reliant on contribution—each partner contributes not only to the work product but to each other's success. Communication surrounds the process—joint planning on the front end, a continual exchange of information throughout, and debriefs at the end of tasks or projects. Conflicts with Collaborative Partners are almost always creative in nature (versus personal), because they are built on the foundation of reliability and trust in the partnership that precedes it. These conflicts are

© 2019 ◯ FINERTY CONSULTING

nonthreatening and seen as a natural and constructive part of the process.

What can you influence with these partners? Small tactical items as well as work products (what to include/not include, what form the work product will take, allocation of responsibilities, etc.). Because there is trust, you can most likely influence their behavior, as well. But more substantial items—things like significant investments or shifts in priorities—may require a bit of added effort.

4. Integrated Partners

At the far end of the continuum are Integrated Partners. Your planning, decisions and problem-solving involve them. You share advice and counsel. Goals are integrated/calibrated, and communication between partners is incorporated into everyday processes. At this level, the partnership may even transcend individuals and be evident at multiple levels in their organizations. You consult and confer on issues that go beyond the obvious connection and business need.

What can you influence with these partners? Really pretty much anything—from behaviors and big-ticket items, like investments and shifts in goals, to smaller tactical issues, like task deadlines and edits in a document. Because trust and knowledge of each other's motivations are high, you can leverage these partnerships by tapping into them to help influence others.

It's probably not a big surprise that as you move to the right of the continuum, influence gets easier, and if the person you need to influence is in the New/Dysfunctional category, your task won't be easy. In order to influence, you need to move your partners out of the New/Dysfunctional box and into a basic place of trust. As you move up the continuum, you can expect greater influence—you will be able to influence on bigger issues, and they will be able to influence you in more significant ways, as well. Second, influence comes most easily when it is matched with the level of partnership; when there is a mismatch, you will either need to work on the partnership or adjust your approach. We'll discuss this more at the end of this section and in Section 4.

Improving partnerships: What are you waiting for?

The key mindset when attempting to move a partnership out of the New/ Dysfunctional box is: **don't wait for them**. In other words—it starts with you. Too often I hear people say their colleague isn't partnering, so they themselves are unable to partner or feel it would be a waste of time to attempt to partner. This is the biggest mistake you can make.

Steve, a former COO, CFO and now C-level consultant, provides a great illustration of the shifts you need to make to your own point of view before attempting any shifts with a partner:

"When I was the division CFO, I got along great with the CEO— Jack, my direct boss. He and I worked wonderfully together. I did not like, nor did I get along with, the corporate CFO, my dotted-line manager—his name was Paul. I don't think he liked me, either, and I just tried to avoid him at all costs. At the goal-setting time one year, the CEO said to me, "Steve, in addition to your accountabilities this year, you are going to be evaluated on your ability to create a relationship with Paul." I said, "Jack, that's the worst thing you can ask me to do. I don't like the guy." Jack knew I didn't like the guy, and he said, "Steve, this isn't about trying to create a relationship. This is about absolutely, without question, doing it. You're going to be evaluated on this the rest of the year." So, that was a direct order, and I did it. I didn't like it. It was difficult at first. But I kept at it, even when Paul didn't reciprocate. I ended up creating a great relationship with him. The net result of that was not only tremendous success for Paul, for me, for the CEO, but also tremendous sales and earnings breakthroughs. And a lot of it came from that relationship that I created with him. Sometimes you have to create relationships even when you don't want to."

Steve demonstrated the "don't wait for them" rule beautifully. He didn't predicate his partnering mindset or behavior on Paul's commitment, values or behavior. In other words, he didn't wait for Paul to change or to initiate improvements—he initiated the process himself.

Steve's boss nudged him into changing his mind about his dysfunctional

 © 2019 ⬠FINERTY CONSULTING

partner, but we don't always have such a force to shift our thinking. Most of the time you will have to dig deep and think differently about the person on your own. If you can't do this, you will not be able to move the partnership. You have to clear your history, which most likely includes all sorts of behaviors, decisions and interactions that have chipped away at trust. You have to replace this history with a simple but powerful thought: "This person is worthy of a partnership." If you have to say it to yourself 500 times a day, it is worth it. Without changing your mind, your actions will be disingenuous and miss the mark.

Making the shift: Seven investments

Partnerships need continual nurturing, and when a partnership is new, dysfunctional or starts to slip backwards, some investment is required. I've outlined seven types of investments you can make to build or rebuild a partnership. You may not need all seven in any given situation, nor is there a single magic bullet—the process is not that simple.

Here are the investments:

Seven Investments

1. TRUST THEM

2. BE TRUSTWORTHY

3. SET/RESET COMMUNICATION

4. CLEAN UP CONFLICTS

5. FOLLOW THE HELP-ME-HELP-YOU RULES

6. ADVOCATE

7. INCLUDE

INVESTMENT #1: TRUST THEM

The mindset of "don't wait for them" comes through loud and clear in terms of this first behavior. You can't wait for the other person to trust you. To build trust, you must trust. Trust begets trust. Lack of trust creates more work for yourself (reviewing, controlling, attending to the extreme) and more work for them (covering, justifying, explaining), which only gets you further from trusting.

But think about what trust does—real, resilient trust is hard to defend against. Have you ever not trusted someone who unconditionally and genuinely trusted you? Said another way, have you ever trusted someone completely and genuinely when they didn't trust you?

Even if it's little things, you will have to start trusting them on something. Without this investment, risky as it may be, the partnership will go nowhere.

Here are a few examples of what "I trust you" looks like:

I don't trust you	I trust you
"I can't be at the meeting, we need to reschedule."	"Go on without me, I don't need to be there."
"I need to see that one more time before I am OK with it."	"I don't need to see it again, go ahead and send it out."
Cc-ing your boss or their boss	Just sending it straight out to them
Holding information until asked	Spontaneously and proactively sharing information
Needing to see it has been done	Assuming it has been done, even when you aren't there to witness it

© 2019 ◯FINERTY CONSULTING

INVESTMENT #2: BE TRUSTWORTHY

Trust is a two-way street. You have to trust them, as well as earn a basic level of trustworthiness, to move out of a dysfunctional partnership or initiate a new partnership. When I asked Steve about where he started with Paul, he said he just started with the bare-bone basics, "I made sure I was reliable and consistent, and when I wasn't, I wasn't afraid to admit it."

Reliability and consistency in a partnership mean simple things like responding to questions, being on time, delivering the work product you said you would, and making decisions that are in line with what you have said and done previously. And when you fail to be reliable and consistent, be upfront about it. The only thing worse than doing something that calls into question your reliability or consistency is failing to acknowledge it. Let's say you are in a meeting, and everyone decides they are going with Option A. Joe, a participant in the meeting, does Option B and doesn't tell anyone—you all find out through the grapevine. The impact of his mistake just expanded exponentially. Not only did he go back on his word (failed to be reliable), he didn't tell anyone (failed to acknowledge). When you act like Joe, people will think that you either didn't see the incongruity or assumed they wouldn't notice—and the second act damages trust even further than the initial one. If you waver on your commitments, be transparent about it or you risk digging yourself deeper into a difficult trust-rebuilding situation.

INVESTMENT #3: SET/RESET COMMUNICATION

There are five steps to establish or recover good communication between partners. Start with the basics. All you need to focus on here (like reliability and consistency in resetting trust) is informing—make sure they get the information they need.

Acknowledge: That your communication may have been lacking in the past and what issues that may have caused (in the case of an existing relationship).

Ask: Ask your partners what they need to know and how they want to find out. Then continue asking whether your communication is working for them.

Plan: Agree on a communication plan that outlines what, when and how.

Get into a rhythm: Cadence in communication is important. A regular rhythm of communication (like weekly emails with a consistent, easy-to-read format or monthly discussions with a set agenda) drives comfort and trust.

Careful of the "out of sight, out of mind" trap: Your partners are likely to be physically scattered. Don't rely on the "who you see" method of remembering what and with whom you need to communicate. Those whom you don't run into are more easily overlooked.

Stephanie told me about some seemingly innocuous check-in meetings that got things back on track with the documentation specialists who supported her project:

> *"I sensed things were slipping, and so I instituted monthly check-ins with them. They insisted they were too busy, but I made sure I kept pushing and asked a lot of questions about what would be helpful for both of us. We went over progress, where we were on different initiatives and what was on the horizon. We brainstormed solutions to issues we had—I almost always walked out with a better way to work with them. It kept us informed, focused and on track in terms of our shared goals and who was doing what. We were all much more ready to be proactive because we were on top of things. After about four cycles, I felt things start to shift. We regained our confidence in each other and even comfort—it just made it easier to get things done."*

   © 2019 ◯FINERTY CONSULTING

Stephanie hit on many of the five set/reset behaviors. She also persisted and focused on making the check-ins meaningful not just for her but for her partners, as well.

What she didn't do was wait for them to admit that they had been lousy communicators too, or to ask her what communication she needed. She just focused on informing and kept doing it. She didn't waste energy identifying their shortfalls, only channelled energy into doing the right thing on her end.

INVESTMENT #4: CLEAN UP CONFLICT

If you are in a dysfunctional partnership, most likely you have been stockpiling. When you stockpile, you don't address a conflict, you store it. Sometimes you sweep conflicts under a rug; other times you accumulate them and then dump them on your partner when you have reached a breaking point. Or maybe you are stockpiling and spreading—telling everyone but the person you have the conflict with.

A former boss of mine, Nancy, was definitely stockpiling with Fran, one of her key partners. They both led large teams and were dependent on each other for success, but conflicts and hard feelings had been piling up and getting in the way of any real progress. Years later, when retelling some of the stories to me, Nancy vividly remembered the problems, confrontations and even specific contentious conversations. At the time she thought it was the right thing to do—at first because she didn't want to rock the boat, later because she had given up hope of fixing things.

Stockpiling is a partnership killer. Even if you are not dumping or spreading the word, you can't hide stockpiling. You may think that what you are holding on to doesn't come out in how/what you communicate, how you make decisions or how you behave in general, but it does.

To reset a dysfunctional partnership, you have to clear the slate—either by truly letting go and forgiving or by clearing the air.

What do you let go and forgive? The things that have low impact today. It may have been a big deal 6 months ago, but if it is not consequential now, let it go. Also let go of things that happened once but aren't indicative of the partnership. You don't have to overtly forgive your partner but mentally delete it. No longer spend any time thinking about it or talking about it. Truly let it go.

Tackle those things that have high impact today—whether they happened once or a hundred times. If it affects current results or trust in the relationship, you need to bring it up in a way that builds the partnership.

New partnerships don't come with a bag full of issues to resolve, but discussing potential conflicts and how to deal with them up front might make sense. It is amazing how a brief comment like "Along the way we will probably disagree on how to manage corporate resources" makes addressing the conflict easy, safe and objective when it actually occurs. The conflict shifts from being a big deal, something that you didn't see coming or that was initiated by one partner, to something you knew would come up, and you are ready to move through swiftly.

INVESTMENT #5: HELP-ME-HELP-YOU RULES

There is a classic line from the movie "Jerry Maguire" that describes another set of baseline investments. Jerry Maguire implores his new client to "help me help you." Cross-functional relationships have a strong customer service component to them. But unlike traditional customer service philosophies, in this case the customer is not always right. Instead, the customer plays a huge role in making the relationships work—the onus for a good customer/provider relationship falls evenly on both sides. Maria, an account rep, shared this story:

> *"I had a proposal that needed to get out to a client and went to the woman that drafts these for me. When I walked up, I could tell she was rushed. After talking to her, I found out that she was indeed under the gun. She told me that she had three proposals to get out that day. I knew mine could wait 24 hours, so I didn't cry wolf and tell her mine was just as urgent. I said, 'Well, you know what, mine can wait until tomorrow; why don't you take care of*

© 2019 ⟳FINERTY CONSULTING

those three, and then let's talk tomorrow.' It was the right thing to do, but it also told her that I don't call everything urgent—and when I do, it's for real."

Maria's experience is a great example of several of the help-me-help-you rules. Here are the rules and what they look like from provider and customer perspectives:

The Help-Me-Help-You Rules	Provider Perspective	Customer Perspective
Don't cry wolf, ever	Don't overstate the degree of difficulty of filling a request	Don't overstate the urgency or importance of your request
Know their business	Know their business and anticipate their needs	Know and respect their processes and deadlines, and make sure your request reflects this understanding. Do not expect them to make exceptions to their rules and processes, especially if your poor planning created the situation.
Co-own any failures	Rarely are there just lessons to be learned on one side only, chances are both the provider and customer have adjustments to make	
Don't assume priorities are known or shared	Don't assume that just because you work in the same organization, your partner already understands your priorities. They may have no knowledge or appreciation of the work that you do outside your relationship with them.	Don't assume that just because you work in the same organization, your partner understands your priorities already. Realize you aren't their only priority: know how your request fits into overall workflow and workload.

INVESTMENT #6: ADVOCATE

Being an advocate means you are your partner's eyes and ears, ambassador and supporter, and they are yours—you go above and beyond merely helping and appreciating or being a good team player:

Good Team Players...	Advocates...
Help out when asked	See when their help is needed and jump in
Solve a problem that is brought to them	See problems and bring them to light for their partner
Thank partners for a great job	Let others know what an outstanding partner they are
Let partners know when things aren't going quite right	Help partners figure out how to fix a problem

The right-hand column outlines some behaviors that have the potential to significantly increase trust between two partners. Advocating is much more proactive than other partnership behaviors and much more hands-on, which is what makes it both more risky and infinitely more potent. It is nearly impossible not to want to partner with someone who is your advocate.

INVESTMENT #7: INCLUDE

I conducted a number of focus groups for a hospital client looking to increase the partnership level (and level of influence) with its physicians. The hospital administrators had made a concerted effort over the previous 12 months to communicate better with physicians, but still felt that they were disconnected. After I talked to 50+ doctors, the answer was simple—in fact, so simple that the administration questioned my

© 2019 ○FINERTY CONSULTING

results. The doctors wanted to be included. They wanted to be part of making decisions, brought into problem-solving. The administration had increased the information going out, so the physicians were informed—but that only got them so far. For the doctors, information wasn't enough. The hospital needed to up the ante—the administration needed to include.

Including people in meetings, involving them in decisions and problem-solving and sharing information tells your partners that you not only trust them, you value them. And the bonus is that this inclusion will also improve the quality of those meetings and decisions.

Matching up partnership level with influence opportunity

In an ideal world, what you have to influence matches up perfectly with the level of partnership. For instance, if you need to secure a considerable investment of funds for a new project, the key stakeholder is an integrated partner. But how often does that happen? Certainly not as often as we would like—and if it did, you probably wouldn't need this book!

When there is a mismatch—your need for influence is bigger than your partnerships—you have three options:

1. Make investments to build the partnership before you influence
2. Leverage other partnerships—tap into others to help you influence
3. Leverage other components of our influence model

The first option is probably the least likely. It takes time to build a partnership, and trying to rush this process to gain leverage can work against you because it seems disingenuous.

Your second option we discussed previously, with the story of Stephanie, Ed and Mary: tap into others to provide perspective and act as an advocate, an ally or a surrogate. This basically requires you to see the influence opportunity as a bit of a chess game, with multiple moves. In this option, you don't start by approaching the decision-maker. You begin by pulling others in to help clear the path or walk the path for you. We often overlook the leverage we have through our partners. A key mindset in influencing cross-functionally is that influence is not a solo endeavor—there are always others who you can and should turn to.

Your final option is to leverage other parts of the model—basically make sure that your knowledge, message and conversation are really, really impactful. We will discuss these issues in more detail in sections 4, 5 and 6.

The real lesson in all of this is that having a broad set of partnerships throughout your organization doesn't just make your work easier—by broadening your influence both directly and indirectly, partnerships are what make it possible.

© 2019 ○ FINERTY CONSULTING

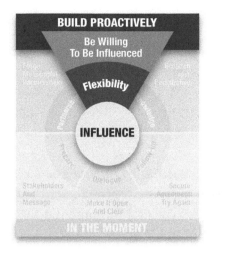

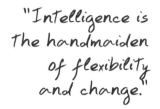

"*Intelligence is the handmaiden of flexibility and change.*"

VERNOR VINGE

Section 2: Flexibility

To Be Truly, Sustainably Influential, You Must Be Willing To Be Influenced

A *research organization I worked with years ago had a group of about 10 highly specialized statisticians providing support to projects and experiments across the organization.* The leaders of the statistical team brought me in because they felt the group didn't "have a seat at the table." And if you aren't at the table, you aren't influencing.

It was perplexing because their skill set seemed pretty obvious. In human resources, where my career roots are, everyone thinks they're an expert. But when you are highly trained in a very specialized area, wouldn't you be brought in on anything remotely associated? Isn't their expertise clear, and clearly different from that of the business folks?

I started by interviewing some of their key partners to understand when and why they invited the statisticians to meetings and brought them in on issues as well as when and why they didn't. The key themes I came away with? "'My way or the highway' mentality," "don't understand anything but their area of expertise—don't get the project needs." The statisticians, stuck in their expertise, had moved from being partners to police.

It's a common trap if you rely on an expertise to provide the basis for your influence, and especially if that expertise is grounded in regulation, legislation, SOP or policy of any type. You become the "no" person—focusing less on collaboration and problem-solving and more on evaluation and veto. After a few rounds of "no," your partners start avoiding you, bringing you in only when absolutely necessary (and usually at the last minute). What they bring you in on is very narrow, and without their broader perspective (more on that in the next section), your influence is limited to small tactical "yes/no" requests. It is a self-fulfilling prophecy.

The other trap we fall into is believing that influence builds with every victory. Every time you get your way, it sets the stage for the next "win." Nothing could be further from the truth. Successive wins, while they feel great at the time, don't always set you up for long-term success.

I call this the jujitsu of influence. Jujitsu is a 2,500-year-old martial art that relies on redirecting the force of your opponent, thereby using his/her energy, not your own. Jujitsu is pertinent to influence because conflict (though generally not hand-to-hand conflict!) is at the heart of influence. Without some level of conflict (or mild disagreement), influence is not necessary. Working cross-functionally, jujitsu looks like stepping away or disarming the conflict by giving concessions. It may seem counter-intuitive and potentially counter to your organization's culture, but it is a powerful approach that leaves your reputation, values and strength intact. Often, stepping back or making concessions on smaller issues or less impactful decisions sets you up to influence on more substantive ideas in the future.

   © 2019 ◯FINERTY CONSULTING

Who influences you?

Flexibility, from a cross-functional influence perspective, means focusing as much on being a target of influence as an agent of influence. This requires *curiosity* to understand others' ideas and opinions when they challenge your own; genuine *openness* to alternative perspectives; *overt recognition* of the value of the other party's input and therefore what they can add to the collaborative venture; and finally, it means *changing your opinion.*

Who has changed your mind at work? In the course I teach on leadership and change, we spend two weeks discussing interpersonal influence, and this is the first question I pose at the start of the module. Several times I have gotten the answer "no one." Then, at least in my head, I direct my lectures and examples to that student. If I can open them up to being influenced, I will make them more influential.

In order to influence, you must be willing—and demonstrate that willingness—to let others influence you. This is especially true in cross-functional work, where relationships are long term and inherently require a lot of give-and-take. When you are steadfast and do more taking than giving in influence situations, your colleagues' trust can dwindle, making it difficult to influence them.

Flexibility ultimately impacts trust—it's a circular relationship:

The more flexible someone is with you, the more you trust them. The more you trust them, the more flexible you are in return.

When I asked our friend Mike, the ER doctor, what he thought his biggest mistake was in his six-month tenure, he told me it was being too "unwavering." When I talked to his partners, they confirmed this. One said something that was particularly interesting. She said, "When he would come to us with something—a new set of requirements or new process to approve—he just didn't budge. He was only in love with his own ideas. It's hard to trust someone who doesn't take input and thinks the only ideas that are good are his. And the more he dug in his heels, the more I felt like I needed to dig in mine!"

I thought about that comment for a long time. I have brought it up in my course on influence quite often. The consensus seems to be that people like Mike, who struggle with flexibility, over time, can lose the trust of others. Think of it from the point of view of the people you're trying to influence. If you consistently see only your side of an issue or only your solution as the right one, how honest are you being? No one is right even 75% of the time. If you aren't honest with yourself, you can't be honest with others—and people start to see that. As we know from Section 1, without trust, there is no influence.

It's no wonder Mike and his partners were stuck. As they saw him to be inflexible, they lost trust and most likely met his inflexibility with their own—which just reinforced his inflexibility. Many cross-functional initiatives and relationships succeed or fail based on a breakdown of this dynamic. We tend to give what we receive and meet their inflexibility with ours.

What does flexibility get me?

Flexibility not only breeds trust, it improves results. When you create a history of willingness to change, others will be inherently more open to change themselves. Our natural human tendency to want to reciprocate kicks in, as does our tendency to give what we receive in terms of the behaviors of others. Robert Cialdini at Arizona State University has done a great deal of research on the science of persuasion, and reciprocity is

© 2019 ⭘FINERTY CONSULTING

one of the six most powerful influence tactics he has identified. More on the other tactics in Section 4, for now we will focus on reciprocity.

Cialdini's research looked at reciprocity in a basic interaction most of us experience probably several times a week—deciding what to tip at a restaurant. You may not think those mints, fortune cookies or other "gifts" make a difference, but Cialdini found that they do. In the experiment, a simple mint increased tips 3%. Giving two mints didn't double but quadrupled the tip increase to 14%. But the biggest jump was when the waiter or waitress left the mint, paused, came back and said, "For you fine people, I'll leave an extra mint." That increased tips 23%! You see reciprocity at work in invitations to social events and favors of all kinds in everyday life. And in our cross-functional organizations, this type of willingness to be flexible—to give—can create a foundation of goodwill that makes you more credible and influential.

What's more, flexibility leads to better decision-making—better outcomes. So what you are proposing has a higher likelihood of being the "right" option.

"If you never change your mind, why have one?"

EDWARD DE BONO

There are two pieces of research that, when linked together, paint an even more detailed picture of the impact of flexibility on influence.

The first bit of research from Pentland et al. (Harvard Business Review, November 2013) looks at the impact of "social exploration"—seeking out a wide range of options and ideas from others (essentially opening oneself up to flexibility and being influenced).

The study showed the power of this openness to change outcomes. Pentland's team gathered data on 1.6 million users of eToro, an investment site that lets day traders see and copy one another's moves. Information on the site is extremely transparent, so the researchers were able to plot the return each trader achieved against the amount of social exploration he or she did. The traders who had the right level of diversity of ideas and people in their networks experienced a return on investment that was 30% higher than the return of the isolated traders. They equally outperformed the traders who were too interconnected to one group and became trapped in an "echo chamber," where similar ideas kept recirculating. What's more, by offering incentives and nudges, the researchers were able to help more traders attain the model idea flow. The results: the profitability of all traders on eToro doubled.

Although these findings involve only stock investments, the researchers believe that many kinds of organizations can apply them to improve their internal decision-making.

The next bit of recent research is from Kupor et al. (Social Psychological and Personality Science, 2014). Previous studies have suggested that people draw inferences about their attitudes and preferences based on their own thoughtfulness, but this one looked at how observing *other individuals* make decisions can shape our perceptions of those individuals and ultimately impact our willingness to be influenced by them. The study found that our assessments of a person's effectiveness and efficiency in making decisions (what they called the degree of "thoughtfulness") affect our openness to be influenced by them.

Pulling together these two pieces of research, we can surmise that being flexible and open makes us better decision-makers, and when we are perceived as better decision-makers, people are more open to our influence.

Remember Stephanie, the project manager mentioned in the Introduction who succeeded where many had failed, thanks to her influencing skills? One of her partners, Rob, gave a great example of how this can play out. Stephanie was trying to influence him to approve a revised approval process for project expenses. In Rob's words, "I knew Stephanie knew her stuff and that she was a good decision-maker for the team. That credibility I had in her really impacted how I felt about what she was

© 2019 ◯FINERTY CONSULTING

proposing—if she thought it was a good idea, I figured it probably was."

Basically, when you influence, you have already decided that this is the right thing to do, and you are attempting to persuade others to reach the same decision. If you are perceived as a good decision-maker, like Stephanie was—based on observations of your decision-making process and outcomes—then others are more likely to be influenced by you. Basically, they trust your judgment and believe that if you reached a certain decision, it was a thoughtful one that you see the credibility of.

Where do you get stuck?

In order to be more flexible, you must know where you get stuck—whom and what you tend to be less flexible with. We tend to fall into patterns here—it may be that there is little a certain person can do to change your mind based on past history. Maybe they haven't proven to be trustworthy or flexible with you. If there is a person, team or function with which you dig in your heels, examine the filter you are viewing their attempts to influence through. Is it fair? Is it based on recent history? Is it applicable in the situation? In Section 1, we discussed not predicating our behavior on the behavior of others and the key mindset of "don't wait for them." Both of those concepts apply here. Begin to challenge your assumptions about them, potentially demonstrate a little flexibility and see how that changes the dynamic. They may be overly steadfast with you because that's the behavior they see from you—if you shift your behavior a few times, they may return in kind.

There might be a topic that you just can't budge on—a pet project, a philosophical belief in how something must be done, a personal perspective or experience you just can't let go of. But the most powerful filter comes from our expertise. Remember the statisticians I introduced at the beginning of this section? We are generally least flexible with what we know the most about. When I discuss flexibility in my workshops, time and time again, people discover that they are least flexible when they are dealing with something that they are an expert on.

Over time, this can turn our expertise into policing. We become inflexible, stuck in our ways. I once had a colleague call it becoming a "purist." You begin to believe so strongly in your area of expertise or the procedures, policies or laws that govern it that nothing less than 100% compliance will do. Once you are in this sort of "police state," people begin to avoid you, and once you are cut out of the process, you lose your chance to influence. Alternatively, they bring you in only when they have to or at the tail end of things, and you have no choice but to police.

Thus, flexibility, as displayed by water, is a sign of life.

Rigidity, its opposite, is an indicator of death.

ANTHONY LAWLOR

I worked for several years with a team responsible for ensuring that all FDA regulations were followed during product research, development, manufacture, distribution, marketing and selling. If you've never worked in an FDA-regulated environment, you get a sense of their requirements when you hear the disclaimers at the end of every TV ad for a medicine. Imagine that level of regulation at every phase of the product life cycle!

The leader of the team was a pretty amazing woman, Bev. She walked into a team that was well established as the regulatory police. They were the "no" people—rigid, tunnel vision with FDA guidelines and regulations as their tools.

Bev was determined to change all that. She set out a vision that her team would be viewed as trusted partners, whose counsel was sought out, not avoided. The team created vision statements, described behaviors, and started rewarding more for partnering and less for driving compliance at all costs.

 © 2019 ⬭FINERTY CONSULTING

The results, over two years, were pretty amazing. By shifting behavior, they definitely upped the partnerships across the organization. But what was really amazing was that compliance didn't take a hit. It's not like they became careless and put the company at risk. They just figured out where they could be flexible and acted on it. With that flexibility, they had the strength to come down hard when they needed to.

If you've noticed that you tend to get stuck in a certain area (your area of expertise or something you have worked with for a long time), you must be hyper-vigilant about knowing when you are in that zone and what your natural tendencies are. If you feel that you are focused mainly on being understood (versus understanding others), you may have slipped into police mode. There are a few things to keep in mind if you find yourself in this state:

Replace those natural tendencies with curiosity.

Curiosity is the enemy of inflexibility: questions are your tool.

Be inquisitive, and imagine you are hearing the complaint, recommendation, idea or request for the very first time. With this mindset, you are likely to hear things differently and to hear different things, which sets you up to be much more flexible.

The balance is in not becoming flexible to the point that you are unreliable. A participant in one of my workshops described this perfectly when she said, "Susan, I came into my new role trying to please everyone, agreeing to everything. Several months in, I had to go back and undo all those camaraderie-gaining agreements. Now I feel like my voice is weakened because if I say, 'This is what we have to do,' they think that all they have to do is wait it out or pretend to agree because I'll change my mind anyway."

Too much wavering and people will stop trusting you—they won't jump on the train with you because they have seen you jump off mid-course too many times.

What about the times I can't be flexible?

At this point you may be thinking, but what about when I can't be flexible? There are absolutely going to be those times. Here's what the best do to stay in the partner zone and out of the police zone:

> *Before you say no, ask a lot of questions. Get to their real need. There may be a way to meet the need in another way.*

> *When you say no, have other ideas. Always follow a "no" with a "but here's what I/we can do that might get you close."*

> *Pick your battles. Know where there is give and where you need to be steadfast. People will respect and trust your steadfastness when it is used sparingly.*

The bottom line is that you have to be willing to be open to change. Without this, trust suffers, partnerships weaken and influence is diminished. In the words of a participant in a recent workshop, "If I'm not willing to be influenced by you or your expertise, I've destroyed the whole power of working cross-functionally."

© 2019 FINERTY CONSULTING

"To know what you know and what you do not know, that is true knowledge."

CONFUCIUS

Section 3: Knowledge

The Most Influential People In The Organization Are The Ones Who Know The Organization Really Well

In the workshop on influence that I teach at the University of Wisconsin-Madison, I do an exercise on perspective. Participants take something they want to influence at work and quickly describe it from their perspective. Often it's a request for funding, milestone change, resources, process changes, etc. Once they've described their own perspective, I ask them to describe it from the perspective of the person they are influencing. Here, they usually struggle. Then I have them partner up with someone else, describe it to their partner and have their partner describe it from yet another perspective. I often threaten to have them go through a fourth round of this, but by three they get it: our perspective is just that—*our* perspective, one perspective. And they are usually pretty taken aback by how many perspectives there are on a fairly simple problem and how easily and quickly they narrowed theirs.

Perspective is a fact of life. Without it we wouldn't have opinions, ideas or recommendations. But when it comes to influence in an organization, it can either work in our favor or against us. When it is broad and includes an understanding beyond your position, team, function or location, it can be very, very powerful. When it is narrow, your ideas can be quickly dismissed as folly.

Two things stand in the way of the powerful, broad perspective that can boost our level of influence. The first is passion—counter-intuitive I know, but hang in there. The second is lack of knowledge. We will focus on knowledge in this section, but first a word on passion and why it can be our nemesis. Passion works in our favor because it provides the impetus to influence. We feel strongly about something—we attempt to change it. Passion is a kick-starter. But it can also cloud our judgment.

I was shocked when my client Ken told me a story of his reaction to a proposed organizational change: "You absolutely cannot do this—it

> "If you change the way you look at things,
> the things you look at change."

WAYNE DYER

will never work in our region, and we refuse to support it!" He had not so calmly exclaimed this to the head of IT, who was trying to centralize resources by pulling his IT resources into a team at headquarters. "I basically did the adult version of a hissy fit," he explained to me later. "Did she move?" I asked, thinking perhaps his organization's culture supported hissy fits as an acceptable form of influence. "Of course not, and I have spent months rebuilding the relationship. I just got so caught up in my own view of it that I couldn't and wouldn't see it from any other angle."

Could Ken have influenced the situation? Who knows. But in this case, not only did he miss a possible opportunity to influence, he damaged a relationship with a partner. And he did it because his passion got the best of him. In influence, passion should be behind every opportunity, but in most cases, putting it out front clouds your perspective and lessens your chances for success.

Although you may not have had an interaction like Ken's, we've all gotten fired up about a change we want or a change we want to prevent. We need an additional resource on a project—why can't they see the need? We want an exception to a policy—how can they be so blind to the business need? Any time we see a need and want to act on it, there is a little (or a lot!) of passion behind it. But if that passion is not backed by perspective, you get yourself in trouble.

So why is perspective so important? Because in our cross-functional up/down/across working world, the target of your influence is most likely in a different function, division or location in the organization than you. That means you cannot assume that you know the impact of what you are influencing on them, their operations and processes, or their team. The chances of creating unintended consequences are high. You have to look beyond your own area to understand the impact and reaction of those on the receiving end. This will prepare you for their possible questions, concerns or objections, and it will tell them that you are thinking beyond your own needs and interests.

What you need to know

Knowledge-building spans both sides of our influence model. It is both something you do on an ongoing basis and something you need to do in the moment—or when you are preparing for a specific influence opportunity. We'll talk about information you need to prepare for your influence conversation in the next section. For now, let's talk about the proactive knowledge-building that is done on an ongoing basis.

So what do you need to know? The keyword is "broad." Your knowledge should reflect an understanding of different parts of the organization; both internal and external perspectives and different components of the organization (formal and informal).

> *"Your perspective is always limited by how much you know. Expand your knowledge and you will transform your mind."*
>
> BRUCE H. LIPTON

If you are not in a revenue-generating part of the organization, you need to know (and prove you know) how the heck the organization makes and loses money. Unfortunately, when you are overhead, you automatically wear the label of "doesn't know the business."

If you are in a headquarters, you need to know the realities, constraints and big-picture priorities of people working in satellite offices, regions, the field—whatever your organization calls it.

If you are in the US, do you understand what it takes to get things done internationally? If you are office-based, do know the challenges faced by manufacturing?

And to all of the above: vice-versa. I could go on and on with these organizational dichotomies, but you probably get my drift. You need to know the organization beyond the tip of your nose. This doesn't mean you have to know every little corner in depth, but for those functions, teams, projects and locations that you work most closely with, you need to build your knowledge and appreciation of their specific needs and challenges.

 © 2019 ◯FINERTY CONSULTING

Building Knowledge

How you build this knowledge ranges from straightforward, low-commitment to more complex and high-commitment investments.

Ask questions. Simply put, reach out and ask questions beyond just the task at hand. For partners, understand their role and realities outside of just how it touches your role and your realities.

Get exposure. Shadow people, visit clients or customers, and see your company's products or services in action.

Move around. The best influencers are those who have walked in others' shoes. Do not be afraid to look at positions outside of your functional/location silo. The credibility (read: influence) that movement will give you—to both your home base and new team—is immeasurable. Purposefully take on assignments that will broaden your knowledge of other parts of the business, build your network, and expose you to different products, operations and teams.

Formal learning. Are there workshops, courses or readings that might help build your knowledge of the organization? Company internal and external websites and social media sites, industry websites and blogs are great sources.

Know the organization

The ideas above are all about gaining an understanding of your partners' realities. But you also need to get to know and understand the organization as a whole so that you can put anything you are influencing into a broader context.

Crucial knowledge here includes:

COMPETITORS

VISION

STRATEGIES

OPERATIONS

KEY CHALLENGES

STRENGTHS, WEAKNESSES, OPPORTUNITIES, THREATS

A great reference for this information is the book *What the CEO Wants You to Know* by Ram Charan. This book provides not only sound general business knowledge, but also helps identify the information you need to gather and be on the lookout for in your own organization.

Know the politics

I know. Politics is a dirty word in organizations, often whispered under the breath. But to be influential, you will have to say it out loud, put it on the table, examine it, plan for it and work it.

Defined broadly, politics is the application of formal and informal power, influence and social ties to get things done. No organization is without this—multiple people all exerting some level of power creates our political atmosphere. It's just human nature. You assemble a group of people with unique personal agendas, competing organizational goals and different experiences, opinions and baggage, and you can't help but create some political strife. We aren't robots. We feel, therefore we politic.

The examination of politics in influence situations starts with a shift in mindset. When you read the heading to this section, what words came to mind? Probably words like "backstabbing," "maneuvering," "posturing"

© 2019 ⬭ FINERTY CONSULTING

and "favoritism." These words are the reason so many of us try to rise above, or pay no attention to politics. We don't want to get our hands dirty.

What if we shift our way of thinking to phrases like "how work really gets done," "informal workings and network of relationships in the organization." Wouldn't you want to tap into that? Thought of this way, politics are not only something you must be aware of to influence, they become another channel for influence.

If we are attempting to influence things that are in the best interest of the team, organization, project, etc., don't we want to use every mechanism available to us? Said another way, aren't there just as many positive ways to tap into the organization's political workings as there are negative?

One of the best resources on organizational politics is Joel DeLuca's book, *Political Savvy*. In it, he posits that negative words like "backstabbing" and "posturing" really only describe one approach to politics. He goes on to lay out eight other possible political "styles."

These styles are created at the intersection of your actions and the degree to which those actions are positive, neutral or negative. Here is a look at each style:

Impact

		Negative	Neutral	Positive
Action	Initiates	Machiavellian	Responsible	Leader
	Predicts	Protector	Speculator	Advisor
	Responds	Cynic	Fatalist	Spectator

Political Savvy, by Joel R. DeLuca

The boxes in the far left hand column describe what you do—do you respond to the politics around you, do you tend to be a bit more active and try to predict political actions or fallout or do you initiate actions associated with organizational politics. The boxes along the top of the table describe the intent and outcome. The words in each of the boxes paint a picture of what that style looks like.

The negative words we associate with politics clearly fall into the aptly named "Machiavellian" bucket. These are your active political animals, out for number one, planning the next move, etc. If there are Machiavellians hovering around whatever it is you want to influence, you will need to be extra diligent in your planning and approach. More on that in Section 4, but in general terms, when you are influencing something, you need to know who your Machs are and have strategies ready to neutralize them.

In reality, and in this model, there are many other approaches. The approaches of "Responsible" and "Leader" indicate people who are active in more neutral or positive ways. DeLuca calls the "Responsible" the white blood cells of the organization. It is these people who look to protect the organization from negative politics. The "Leader" actively tries to align personal and organizational goals and to help people potentially see things differently.

For our conversation on influence, I want to focus on one box—the "Advisor." As the name indicates, this person seeks to be savvy enough to advise others. These are your lynchpins when influencing—it is these people who can help you identify the political landscape and possible Machiavellians and can guide you on how to navigate potential pitfalls.

If you have never had an advisor, you may not truly understand their power. I will never forget an outing my then boss took our team on. One morning, before the team-building session began, she took me and a colleague for a walk through the woods—literally and metaphorically.

For an hour she schooled us on the power struggle around ownership of a large organizational initiative between our team and another team (led by a Mach). Very unemotionally and objectively she laid it out. In a bit of shock, but still curious, my colleague and I asked a million questions about this situation and the history of conflicts between our two teams. This was a woman close to retirement, very successful, not

© 2019 ◯ FINERTY CONSULTING

bitter at all with what was happening around her but who wanted her two highly promising yet incredibly naïve employees to get a glimpse of and prepare for life at the next level.

"It is what it is," she said, "and you just need to be aware, you need to have your radar up for this—not just for this team, but overall. And you don't have to play their game—you can rise above it, but 'rise above it' doesn't mean ignore it or pretend it doesn't exist."

For me, that conversation shed light on things that had been a mystery—behaviors that seemed out of place, decisions that seemed more painful than they needed to be. From there on out, I realized that if I wasn't seeing this landscape—with all its minefields, unmarked trails and terrain, there was no way I was going to be able to navigate it.

And that is the second key point about influence and politics. Not playing the game is not an option—but you can play it on your own terms with your own good intent. Ignoring the game is also not an option. The most influential people are politically savvy. Burying your head in the sand is never a good influence tactic. To be influential, you must see the landscape—and constantly fill in any gaps in your knowledge of it. This helps you understand what can be influenced, what can't, whom to influence and how. The mindset required is to accept that politics are always present—be aware and be wise. In DeLuca's words, being politically savvy is influencing: ethically build a critical mass of support for an idea you care about.

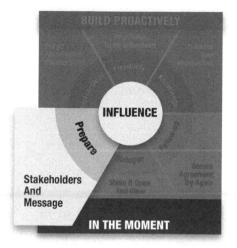

"One important key to success is self-confidence. An important key to self-confidence is preparation."

ARTHUR ASHE

Section 4: Prepare

Influencing Cross-Functionally Is Never A Straight Line, There Are Almost Always Multiple Stakeholders And Scenarios To Prepare For

Before we try to influence something, it is absolutely critical that we slow things down just a bit to consider if we should influence it at all, decide who we should be influencing and think through the conversation. Without these steps, we are almost guaranteed to run after things that aren't worth our time, waste time talking to people who aren't the real decision-makers and approach the problem in a way that is restricted to our own narrow perspective. This section lays out this process in detail.

Within the first five minutes of meeting Stephanie, our project manager from the Introduction, I could tell she was one of those people who nothing could rattle; faced with conflicting demands, competing priorities and influence opportunities that would intimidate most, she was able to stay focused.

I asked her about this, and she immediately referred to her organization's approach to prioritizing—a ranking system, which, while interesting, didn't quite answer my question.

"There must be countless things you need to influence—from milestones to resources to decisions of all sorts. Not to mention the small things like conversations that need to take place, issues that you need others to resolve. How do you manage all that coming at you? How do you know what to influence?"

Her response was telling. "I just go in assuming that I will see a lot—I have pretty strong radar—but that I don't have to take it all on. I figure out what I can get traction on, and drop or hand off things I know I need but can't get traction on. I just never assume that if I see it I have to influence it. Sometimes it just makes sense to let something play out or let someone else influence it."

Counter that with Mike. In addition to coming to terms with the fact that his unwavering "influence style" was costing him, he realized he was going after too many influence targets at once.

When I interviewed him as part of my research for *Master the Matrix*, he shared an exhausting laundry list of all the things he was trying to influence. "Shared" is probably too nice a word—since we knew each other from teaching at Northwestern, he really did something more like "dumping." At the end of all this, I asked him, "Mike, you're an ER doctor—you know how to triage, right?"

If you aren't familiar with the word, "triage" is a medical term that refers to the process of efficiently prioritizing patients based on the severity of their condition when resources are insufficient to treat them all immediately. It comes from the French verb *trier*, meaning to separate, sort, sift or select. This is a way of life for an ER doctor. But Mike had

 © 2019 ⓒFINERTY CONSULTING

completely left that concept by the wayside when he had to prioritize influence opportunities, rather than medical issues.

I went on to explain the mindset of viewing influence as a muscle that should be flexed only where it's really needed. Attempting to influence everything you see that needs to change can actually make you less influential.

Influence as a Muscle

The most influential people treat their influence as a muscle and exert it with prudence.

Think about an average day at your job. Even if you don't realize it, you probably have the opportunity to influence something not just daily, but minute to minute. Timelines, resource allocation, budgets, policies, strategies and even individual behaviors are all open to being influenced at some point—probably not just in one direction but up, down and across the organization.

Stephen Covey begins *The Seven Habits of Highly Effective People* with the concept of Circle of Influence/Circle of Concern.

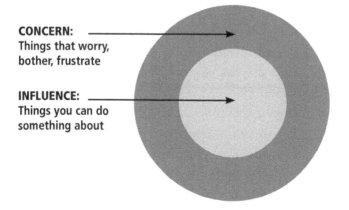

CONCERN:
Things that worry, bother, frustrate

INFLUENCE:
Things you can do something about

In Covey's description, among the decisions that enter your consciousness, there are some you can do something about and others you can't. His advice is to focus on those you can influence and let the others go—don't let them take up your time or energy.

When roles and teams are built around critical initiatives or critical customers, there is no shortage of things that need to be influenced. It can be overwhelming, especially when you don't have the luxury of playing the title card. This can do funny things to your influence muscle. You can easily fall into one of two traps:

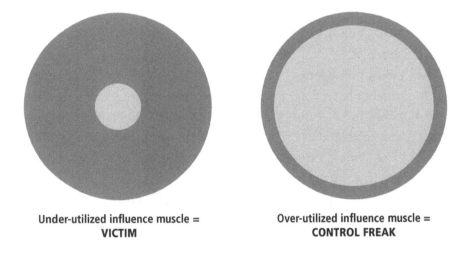

Under-utilized influence muscle =
VICTIM

Over-utilized influence muscle =
CONTROL FREAK

For some, the broad perspective and lack of formal power that are characteristic of today's organizations can become overwhelming, and they go into victim mode, convincing themselves that they are powerless and blaming the organization, project or boss for everything. Others attempt to corral and control everything to gain comfort, which is exhausting, dilutive and builds up resentment from the stakeholders around them. By overusing their influence, they become like that billboard you see every morning on your way to work—attention-grabbing at first, but eventually just blending in with the scenery.

This is a key mindset: treat influence as a muscle. Strengthen it and do things to maintain it every day. If you don't want to overuse or overexert the muscle, you will have to triage, but also be careful not to become a

 © 2019 ⟲ FINERTY CONSULTING

victim and underuse the muscle, because then it will atrophy.

Deciding to wield your influence muscle

You should clearly act on issues that are within your sphere of influence and have a high impact on your team and/or project. By the same token, those issues that are not within your influence and have a low impact should be left by the wayside. But there are plenty of variations in between. Here is a way to think about triaging items that enter your Circle of Concern:

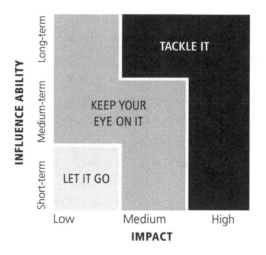

The idea here is that you have a range of options—from completely letting go to charging ahead at full throttle. Understanding this range helps you keep a balance. When you are triaging, be sure to challenge your historic boundaries. In a situation where your automatic assumption is that you can't influence, think again about what you could possibly do. If the issue is something that historically you have tackled but with mixed results, skip it and see how the situation plays out without your influence. Also, watch for items to shift, either in terms of their impact or your influence level, and readjust accordingly.

Stephanie was great at picking her battles. She had good instincts about which battles were realistically "worth it" and consulted others when she wasn't sure. She focused on the critical issues and let others run their course. In her words, "It is amazing the power of letting things play out. Sometimes my biggest influence was when I chose to step aside and watch what happened." Doing this not only helped Stephanie triage, conserve energy and stay focused, it also helped her practice the "Influence Jujitsu" we discussed earlier in Section 2.

So you think you should Influence—What's next?

I was once given the dubious task of "facilitating" my division's monthly senior leadership meetings with Dave, the president of the division, and his 10 direct and dotted-line reports (I reported to one of the team members). Dave loved these meetings; everyone else dreaded them. They were described as "talking heads giving updates on stuff that could have been emailed to me." No strategic talk, no problem-solving—actually little interaction whatsoever. The team decided "it would be great" if I could "fix" the meetings. After attending one, I vehemently agreed that they needed fixing.

I got time on the president's calendar the following week, supposedly to "talk" about the issue. I opened with the fact that the team wasn't getting much out of the meetings, and based on what I had observed, I had a solution that could make them more meaningful. After five minutes of this "talk," he nodded politely, said he'd think about it, thanked me for my time and stopped just shy of patting me on the head on the way out the door. Being escorted out after five minutes is a pretty sure sign that influence just plain didn't happen.

My experience is a great example of what can happen when you have little or no preparation. We often grab hold of an idea, fall in love with it, think everyone else will feel the same and then just storm the Bastille—hoping that our passion, mixed with theirs, will make the influence inevitable.

 © 2019 ⊙FINERTY CONSULTING

The good news is that I recovered pretty quickly, as we'll see later in this section. We'll start with analyzing and planning around the "who" of this phase—your stakeholders. Then we will move to planning your message.

Your Stakeholders

So you have something that needs influence, you've taken it through some triaging questions, and you're ready to start. Your first question is, "Who?" From there, you begin to determine what type of stakeholder they are, how important they are, and then look at the best way to influence them.

As I have mentioned before, influence in most organizations is a bit of a chess game. There is a network of people, closely knit together, and the moves of one impact another. You need to be able to see this chessboard to determine whom you need to influence, and it is almost always more than one person.

Think of stakeholders at three different levels:

Stakeholders. The outside of the circle includes people who need to support and give input.

Starting Point Stakeholders. This next level is your opening move—the person you attempt to get on board first. They may be able to help you get your decision-maker and others on board or they may be a naysayer who you want to "quiet" quickly so they don't derail things. Or they may fall into the categories of influence support we talked about in Section 1:

Perspective   Advocate   Ally   Surrogate

Often we are in a rush to get to the decision-maker and bypass this step. Big mistake. This stakeholder step is critical to build momentum, form alliances and practice your message.

Ultimate Stakeholder. This is your destination—the person you need on board to get the decision made, the idea adopted, etc.

There may be times when you can go straight to the decision-maker, especially if he or she is someone you know well, or the issue or idea is straightforward. But again, pausing to consider if there are others to bring in or get input from can build momentum when the situation is a bit more complex or involves some unknowns.

In applying this to my situation, I fell into the common trap of going straight to the decision-maker. I didn't even consider pulling in others to get input on my ideas or perspective on Dave—whom I hardly knew.

In this situation, the stakeholders would be the people on Dave's team. When I was sent back to the drawing board after my five minutes with Dave, I reached out to a few of them. Doing this helped me build understanding of the situation and buy-in for my solution. It also helped identify who the next-level stakeholder should be.

Through this due diligence, I learned that Abby, a member of the team who had a long history with Dave, was really passionate about

© 2019 ◯ FINERTY CONSULTING

the meetings. I also found out that Abby had a lot of pull with Dave. Abby became my opening move. She provided perspective on Dave—his preferences, hot buttons and motivations.

For me the obvious ultimate stakeholder was Dave—they were his meetings. But it isn't always that obvious. In some cases, the decision-maker may not become clear until you begin the process of discussing the idea and reaching out to starting point stakeholders.

YOUR STAKEHOLDERS: WHERE DO THEY STAND?

Going into any conversation, you want to have a sense of (or be prepared to get a sense of) where the stakeholder stands on your idea and how much impact they may have on getting your idea or proposal approved. When you consider these two dimensions, you can really begin to see what you need to do with them. Some may be right where you need them. Some may need to be moved because they could easily delay or completely derail your efforts. Still others fall in between. Think about this as a way to triage your stakeholders—a way to prioritize and sequence your consensus-building approach:

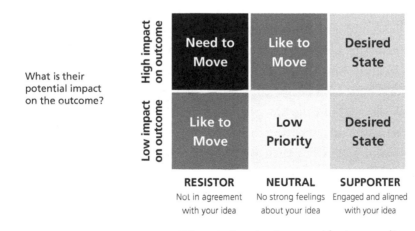

This helps you triage how you manage your time. Those who are neutral and have low impact are lower priority—you don't necessarily have to spend a lot of time working to get them on board. Your time can be focused on the people who you need to move or would like to move. Thinking of it this way also helps you determine how you can use different stakeholders in the process. A stakeholder in the "Desired State" can help move other stakeholders who you need on board.

YOUR STAKEHOLDERS: UNDERSTANDING THEIR PREFERENCES

There are also two key preferences you need to understand about your stakeholders: (1) how they like to take in information and (2) how they make decisions.

The first is easy—are they an email communicator or do they like to talk things through? Do they like to see information/ideas ahead of time and prepare for conversations or do they like to be walked through the information and discuss more off the cuff? You may already know this, and if you don't, ask people who have influenced this stakeholder in the past. In thinking about Dave, based on my limited exposure, I knew he was an in-person kind of guy—so that part I actually got right in my first pass at influencing him.

The second is a little trickier, but it's even more important. Ultimately, you want this person to make a decision to support your idea. So you need to know how they typically make decisions. Are they a bottom-line, numbers person? A big-picture visionary? Or more of an imitator—they follow the lead of others?

Gary Williams and Robert Miller do a great job of describing decision-making styles in their book, *The Five Paths to Persuasion*, which is based on a two-year project studying the decision-making styles of more than 1,600 executives across a wide range of industries. I've taken some artistic license and simplified their model to apply it to cross-functional influence.

 © 2019 ◯FINERTY CONSULTING

	Description	Be Prepared to Address
Innovators	These are people who love a new idea; they are interested more in the solution than the problem and like a big-picture hook. Light on details, until they have a good grip on the broader perspective. Love to inspire and be inspired.	How this fits into bigger strategy How this is different from previous approaches
Imitators	They want to know who else is doing it and how this is similar to what has been done before. Not risk takers, slower to decide.	People, teams and organizations that have already tried this How this is similar to problems and solutions previously encountered How you will mitigate risk
Analytics	Facts, figures, bottom lines and lots of detail are what drive their decisions. Light on the bigger picture, until their detailed questions are answered—and they ask many.	The details of the problem and solution Quantitative impact and evidence
Hands-On	They love their own ideas and need to have their fingerprints on the idea; they will buy in if it is their idea and/or they can control the solution.	Ideas and not plans, options What is open, undecided and under their control, and where they can give input.

We tend to assume that everyone makes decisions in the same way that we do, and so we influence in that very same way. I tend to be on the Innovator side—I love new ideas and big-picture thinking. I will never forget trying to sell a client on a new workshop approach that I had fallen in love with. Using words like "cutting edge," "innovative," "new" and "different," I proceeded to only fall further in love with the idea myself. My client, who I later learned was an Imitator, had eyes glazed over, and when I finally took a breath, he calmly asked, "Could you give me the names of people that have done this before?" I took the entirely wrong approach and never heard from him again.

And it wasn't very different when I attempted to influence Dave. I designed what I thought was a super innovative way to structure and conduct his meetings—cutting edge! Role model for the organization! Dave was the president of a $7 billion business. Innovative meetings were not a business necessity for him. He grew up in the Sales ranks. He was a bottom-line financial guy—an Analytic.

We've talked about the power of perspective (theirs—not yours!) in Section 3, and how you have to be able to see and prove you see the idea or issue from the perspective of the person you're trying to influence. You also have to put yourself in their shoes when determining your overall approach, sequencing and presentation of the information.

Your Message: The Frame

The "frame" is the first two to three sentences that position what you are asking for. There are many possible frames for any given issue. Do you frame it as a problem or an opportunity? As an investment or an expense? Do you frame the current situation or the solution? A new product to consider or a chance to step into a new market?

Let's return to my story. After my epic fail, I went back to the drawing board. I got input from my stakeholders and started to put numbers to the problem to get to Dave's analytic side. Being in HR, I was able to gather salary information and calculated hourly rates of the 12 participants, time spent in the meetings and travel to the meetings (half of the group traveled in from outside the country). I also calculated expenses for travel and for things like catered meals during the meeting. Then I took a look at the agendas for the past year and saw that they were spending over 90% of the time in those meetings listening to presentations. I also got Abby to agree to be my advocate.

I dropped Dave an email with the dollar figure and percentage of time spent listening to presentations versus discussion. I also dropped Abby's name. I heard back from him almost immediately. His response?

 © 2019 ○FINERTY CONSULTING

"Susan! Where did you get those numbers? We've got to do something about these meetings!"

I changed my frame from, "Your people aren't getting much out of these meetings, and here's what I think is a solution" to "I did some number crunching, and it looks like you are spending $50,000 per month on the leadership team meetings, where more than 90% of the time is spent listening to presentations. Just checking to see if this was your intended investment?" Reframing the problem got his attention. Once I had his attention, the influence was easy.

Jeffrey Pfeffer, in *Managing with Power,* gives a lot of weight to how we frame an issue: "Establishing the framework within which issues will be viewed and decided is often tantamount to determining the result."

We often tend to frame things in one way—our own. Especially at first. Just like me, your first frame is almost always wrong. I framed the meeting issue as I saw it: a problem with the level of engagement. That got me polite disregard. Framing from the recipient's point of view can get their attention right from the start.

I have found in workshops that when you start to frame an issue, just saying it out loud can help you hear if you are stuck in your own perspective. Saying it out loud to another person (and not talking to yourself!) provides great insight, as well.

Here are the keys to framing the issue or idea you are trying to influence:

Frame the issue in a way that is meaningful to your target. The first thing to do when you are establishing how you will frame the issue is to take the perspective of your target. Sean, a participant in my research, tells a great story of influencing people to make difficult personnel decisions:

> *"When I tried to influence new hiring managers to deal with problem performers, I came up against brick walls because they were afraid to hurt someone's feelings. It wasn't until I reframed it away from 'you need to get rid of this problem performer' to 'you need to*

do what is fair for the other team members who are picking up the slack' that they usually agreed to take action."

I did this when I reframed things for Dave. My initial frame was all around the team not really getting much out of the meetings. My reframe, around the financials, made it meaningful to him and hit his decision-making style, as well.

Here's how I might have framed my idea in a way that hits on the four decision-making styles we discussed earlier:

Innovator: "I've got an idea for an entirely new way to approach these meetings that I think will really help us align the discussions to where we are taking the business."

Imitator: "I've been looking at how I have seen other leadership teams structure their monthly meetings, and I have some thoughts on how it might apply to ours."

Analytic: "I did some number crunching, and it looks like you are spending $50,000 per month on the leadership team meetings, where the bulk of time is spent listening to presentations. Just checking to see if this was your intended investment?"

Hands-On: "There seems to be consensus on the team that we could structure the meetings differently. I am wondering what observations and ideas you have or things you would like to see us try?"

Frame it in a larger context. You have to understand the bigger organizational context before you frame it. Business acumen is a key influence ingredient. Articulate how a change impacts the big picture outside your piece of the organization. In my example, I initially framed the leadership meetings in terms of what they meant to the participants, which was

© 2019 ◯ FINERTY CONSULTING

too narrow for Dave. When I positioned the meetings in the context of his division's investment decisions, I got his attention.

Be specific. One of the biggest mistakes that I see people make is to bury their reason for approaching a person. Consequently, their influence target (especially if they are in upper management) becomes impatient, lost or tunes out. In your frame, indicate, even at a high level, what you want from them. And if you can (without using too many words, this is just your opening statement), say more than "I need your support." Often we stop at this—just a vague request for support—and people don't know what you are asking of them. So they may nod their head at the end of the meeting, but nothing happens because they weren't sure what "support" was supposed to look like! A statement like, "I am looking for your support in presenting this idea to the Steering Committee on the team's behalf," tells them exactly what your "ask" is and makes it more likely they will follow through on your request.

Frame it objectively. One of the leaders involved in *Master the Matrix* told a wonderful story of a country manager from Italy. Each time he started down a path he wanted others to follow, he opened with, "In my country…" He was given feedback letting him know that this influence tactic wasn't working. Framing the situation this narrowly, from only his perspective, immediately put others on the defensive and undermined the credibility of his view. So he switched to, "In a country like mine…" Although he changed his wording, he still missed the point. To influence cross-functionally, take it out of your personal context whenever possible. This shows that you are influencing in the right direction and for the right reasons, and it makes your attempt more credible.

If you are in front of multiple stakeholders at once, all with different needs, you have to think about your frame a little differently. Your goal is two-fold. Catch the attention of the most influential person in the room (hit their needs and decision-making style), while indicating to the others that you'll hit on their interests also.

Let's take a hypothetical detour with my story. Let's say my attempt to influence changing the meeting started with Dave along with several members of his team. And in addition to Dave, who was Analytic, I had some Imitators and Hands-On thinkers to contend with, as well. My frame might sound something like this: "I did some number crunching, and it looks like you are spending $50,000 per month on the leadership team meetings, where over 90% of time is spent listening to presentations. I've got some ideas based on what others are doing, but we have a lot of room for ideas and input from all of you."

Your Message: Your opening point

Once your frame opens things up, now it's time to really lay out your argument. For your first point, you have a couple of choices.

Start with your strongest point. This might be the one with the strongest evidence, proof or impact. It gets their attention and establishes the idea as legitimate. For my situation, I hinted at this in the frame—the financial impact of the meetings. My first point would continue this line of reasoning and give further detail: "The meetings are a significant amount of money and time each month, more than half a million dollars a year, and there is very strong consensus amongst the team that they are not bringing value. What is your reaction to that level of investment given the value derived?"

Start with your strongest point of *agreement*. It might make sense to start with where you have agreement with the stakeholder or stakeholders, especially if there is little agreement elsewhere. Starting here builds some goodwill and rapport with the stakeholder. This place of agreement can be not only your starting point, but a place you go back to. For me, it might have been, "I know we all agree that we need to meet on a regular basis—it's right for the team, and it's right for the business. The time we spend in discussion is critical for moving our initiatives forward. Agreed?"

 © 2019 ◯FINERTY CONSULTING

Start with your strongest point of *disagreement*. If you have a serious point of disagreement, you might want to start there. Call out the elephant in the room. If you don't do this, you risk people listening to each of your points with a "Yeah, but…" precursor in their heads. Here's how I might have used this as a first point, "I know everyone's biggest concern is the time it will take to plan, structure and prepare for these meetings on a monthly basis. I've broken down the time commitment for team members as well as support staff, and it looks like this…"

Start with what you are flexible on. If you are working with stakeholders who want some control or feel like you are dictating, start with an element of your proposal that you are most flexible on. Like starting with a point of agreement, it sets the tone and builds goodwill and rapport. For example, I could have started with, "I've got some specific ideas on structure, but one place I think we have some play is with the length of the meetings."

Your Message: Influence tactics

When we think of how we are going to persuade, we think about facts, statistics, logic and rationale. But some of the most compelling research on influence and persuasion argues that we are missing the point—that humans are hard-wired to make decisions in anything but a logical way!

Our brains are still driven by primitive needs like resource security and social inclusion, which can sometimes make us resistant to being influenced by even the soundest of arguments or, conversely, can make us vulnerable to persuasion by people who are skilled at tapping into the right psychological motivators, whether or not it's in our best interest.

Robert Cialdini's book *Influence: Science and Practice* outlines six fundamental principles of persuasion that anyone can learn and apply to be more effective influencers. These principles allow us to tap into our basic human drives in predictable ways.

Here's how I apply Cialdini's work, as well as others, in cross-functional influence. I break it down into five basic tactics that get beyond just presenting facts.

Identifying Concerns: Humans have a powerful need to be heard and understood. In fact, when we don't feel heard and understood, we often shut down. Once shutdown occurs, influence stops. In order to influence, you have to demonstrate that you have done the work to understand, anticipate and account for the concerns of your influence target. This "clears the air" for them to listen to your idea.

Bargaining/Reciprocity: This is where flexibility comes into play. Think about the trade-offs and currency you may have with your stakeholders. If you have a history of flexibility, they may already be in a position to reciprocate. If not, what can you do in the moment to bargain and adjust to their needs?

Common Vision: Can you paint a picture of what could be? What "fixed" might look like? What that extra resource, extra two months, extra $50,000 might mean? Describe it for them—in detail. What are people doing, what impact are they making? Often, we have this picture in our head but don't share it with others. When they buy into the vision, you can then move them to buying into the tactic or idea you are presenting.

Social Proof: Who else is doing this? What other companies, teams in the organization or people are implementing this or in support of this? People love to be in good company, especially in the company of those like them and those they admire.

Expertise: We talked about how expertise can sometimes limit our flexibility, but expertise does have its place in influence. Kept in check, you can absolutely apply your own expertise in an influence situation, but don't overlook bringing in outside expertise. Whether from outside or from another part of the organization—remember that influence is not

© 2019 ⬭FINERTY CONSULTING

a solo endeavor. You don't get extra points for doing it all on your own.

As you probably already realize, these principles correspond nicely with the different decision-making styles. Identifying concerns is necessary for all types; let's look at the others. Each of the influence tactics are labeled "good, better, best" with regard to how effective a tactic might be for these types of decision-makers or "caution" if this tactic might have some risk for a certain decision-making type.

	Innovator	Imitator	Analytic	Hands-on
Bargaining / Reciprocity	**Good:** Flexibility can help build consensus but in itself won't sell an idea.	**Caution:** Minimize their sense of risk-taking.	**Better:** Situate the benefits of the idea within a broader scope.	**Best:** The trade-offs and your flexibility give them control.
Common Vision	**Best:** They will need to see how your idea fits in with something bigger.	**Better:** Anticipating wide-ranging support can help instill confidence in the idea.	**Caution:** Don't go here until they have their heads wrapped around the details.	**Good:** Big picture can convey the value of an idea but also reduce their sense of ownership over decision-making.
Social Proof	**Caution:** They like to be cutting edge, so they may be turned off by the fact that others have done this.	**Best:** They will want to hear what everyone else is doing.	**Good:** Previous results can help support your idea but need to stand on their own merit.	**Better:** Knowing what has been done in the past can help them reach their own conclusion.
Expertise	**Better:** Expertise can add support to the potential promise of new ideas.	**Good:** Focus on how things have been done in the past, not blazing new trails.	**Best:** Your direct expertise or the expertise you gain from facts and figures will influence them.	**Caution:** Leave them room to feel that they are reaching their own conclusions.

You may never use all of these, but your should consider all of them and then sequence them into your dialogue in a way that builds consensus and agreement.

The important message for this phase of the model is to pause and think strategically. We have a need or a great idea that seems so obvious and perfect and plausible…to us. And because of this we plow through influence quickly, assuming people will "get it" and jump on board once they just hear you out and understand. We fool ourselves into thinking that all we need to do is inform, as opposed to influence. Not everyone is where you are, and slowing down to think through who you need to talk to and how to go about it will help you influence them.

After finishing this section, you may be saying to yourself, "There is no way I have time to do all this." Here are a couple thoughts to consider. First, as I mentioned in the Introduction, we are slowing this process way down to gain insight. Once you go through this a few times, some of these assessments will come pretty quickly. Second, the fact of the matter is that there will be some bigger things to influence that require you to do each of these steps. The mindset in these cases is "slow down to go fast." Slowing down in the preparation phase most likely means you are going to pick up speed in the dialogue and execution phase.

© 2019 ◯ FINERTY CONSULTING

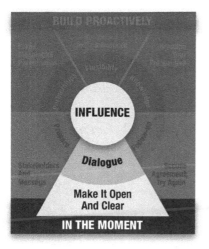

"A conversation is a dialogue, not a monologue. That's why there are so few good conversations: due to scarcity, two intelligent talkers seldom meet."

TRUMAN CAPOTE

Section 5: The Dialogue

The Dialogue Is Truly The Culmination Of The Credibility You've Built Over Time And The Preparation You've Done

Stephanie, whom we have been following in previous sections, didn't always get everything right. When I shifted the conversation from how she influences to the influence behaviors she's seen in others, she told this story about a struggle with role clarity—which happens often when you are working cross-functionally. Here's how she described it:

Karen set up time with me, walked into my office and said that we had a problem to solve. She said that it felt like we were stepping on each other's toes and that our working relationship felt "clunky." She asked if I was *feeling the same, and I said I was. Despite some early work on defining who did what, we were still tripping over each other.*

She asked me how I thought this was affecting our steering committee and our project teams. We both agreed that it was causing confusion and duplication of effort from multiple perspectives. She then pulled out the role document that she and I had worked on six months ago—it outlined who does what in terms of providing information and support on the projects.

In that moment, I realized it was my bad. I was causing this disruption. I was totally and completely breaking every ground rule we had set up. Oops! Be it ego or perceived gains in efficiency, I was bypassing this agreement.

Had Karen walked in, guns blazing, protecting her turf, I would have felt like I had to defend myself. And this thing would have headed south fast. But she didn't present it that way at all. She walked in and laid it out in such a way that I saw what was happening, and I was in the right frame of mind to solve the problem with her.

She was basically influencing me—trying to get me to recommit to the agreement we had in place. She could have just thrown the document in my face and told me to knock it off. But she didn't—she finessed it, and she influenced me. She didn't just get me to comply, she got me to own it. Which, I guess, is where real influence lies?

Indeed, that's where real influence lies. Rarely are we trying to just seek compliance. Compliance means doing something because you think someone is watching. In most of our attempts at cross-functional influence we want people to *want* to do what we are asking. Strong-arming is an influence tactic, but it's not a sustainable approach—it gets old pretty fast, and we fall into policing pretty quickly.

To achieve true influence, you have to have the right mindset. The dialogue needs to be based in the assumption that at the heart of it is a conflict, the "who" in that conflict is most likely a partner, and the outcome is some level of ownership.

© 2019 ○FINERTY CONSULTING

Components of an Influence Dialogue

In the influence dialogue, you introduce or frame the issue and work to have a constructive talk about what you want to accomplish and why. You will have to consider both the issue at hand and the relationship when you enter the conversation—you are aiming for wins on both sides. You may not always get wins, but going in with anything less in mind will undercut your approach. There are three basic components to managing an influence dialogue and working through the resistance you will encounter: (1) include and engage the person you are trying to influence, (2) work to keep them in the conversation, and (3) be clear, succinct, summarize and synthesize.

Each of these three is challenging when we are passionate about what we are trying to get across. Remember in Sections 2 and 3, when we talked about the fact that passion, a necessary ingredient for influence, can get in our way sometimes? Nowhere do we feel it more than when we are in a dialogue with someone. We must constantly fight the urge to do all the talking, get caught up in the moment, miss their nonverbal cues and get lost in too much detail.

Here's a look at each of the three basic components:

Include and engage. Simply put, people adopt ideas more quickly and integrate them more fully when they have been involved in them. The same is true of influence. People are more open to influence when you don't come to them with a *fait accompli.* This is not always possible; there are times when you need someone to do something very specific that has no gray around it. But when possible, walk in with some wiggle room and opportunity for them to put their fingerprints on the decision. Going in softer, with less defined needs, can work to your advantage in influencing (as well as likely improve your solution). Stephanie's opening story is a great example of this. Her partner Karen didn't walk in pointing to the role document as the solution—although I am sure she knew that was the solution! Instead, she walked in ready to explore and problem-solve.

Work to keep them in the conversation. At the heart of influence is conflict, and people don't have the courage, appetite or sometimes the aptitude for conflict to stay in a conversation. They quit too soon—the minute they hear resistance, they retreat. Or they hear resistance, and they dig in their heels even more and begin to defend.

Keeping yourself and the other person in the dialogue is critical. One matrix leader I talked to called this the organizational equivalent of "never go to bed angry." Keep the conversation going until you both decide to shelve it. Pauses and walkaways are good, but come back to the issue and make sure you both decide when the exchange is complete.

The mindset to adopt here is that you are the watchdog of the conversation dynamic, and there are things you can do when people shut down, resist or refuse. When you see and hear signs of this, take responsibility for steering it back on track.

Let's go back to Stephanie and Karen's conversation. Here are a few things Karen could do—and probably did—to help both of them stay in the conversation:

Keep the relationship front and center. Influence dialogues require the relationship to be front and center. Reminding yourself of this fact changes your tone and the words you choose. Reminding them elevates your dialogue to common ground.

> *"I am committed to being a valuable partner with you on this and the other initiatives we have ahead of us—neither of us can do our jobs without the other."*

Listen and acknowledge what they are saying. Once people sense that you aren't listening, you've lost them. There is an incredibly strong human need to be heard and understood—and when you feel you aren't, it's all you can think about. They become defensive of their idea, determined to be heard instead of determined to work with you on the issue. People who are heard open themselves up to influence. Their questions are also valuable, in-the-moment data for you. What are they

© 2019 ○FINERTY CONSULTING

unclear about? What is holding them back from being influenced? What do they care about? This is exactly the type of information that you need to be influential, and you can't get it if you're talking all the time.

"It sounds like you are feeling a bit of the pain of our role overlaps, too."

Restate the big picture and your common ground. When people start to sound defensive or agitated, take a step back and restate your bigger objective and what you have in common.

"There's no doubt we both want to make sure that the client gets what they need as effectively and efficiently as we can."

State what you are *not* saying. When people feel threatened, they may take your comments to the extreme and begin to react to that extreme, as opposed to your actual proposition.

"I am not suggesting that everything we have been working on feels clunky—but there are definitely a few spots that we need to look at ironing out."

Reinforce your ability to reach agreement. Even when things get contentious, retain your optimism for reaching agreement and communicate that with the person you are talking to.

"I think between the two of us we can land on which parts of the role document still make sense and which ones we can potentially edit and improve."

Be clear, succinct, summarize and synthesize. Working cross-functionally is complex, and those who simplify, succeed. Simplicity drives agreement. Reaching an agreement is dependent on your ability to simply and clearly state what is needed and why. If there are options to consider, they must be laid out clearly. Overwhelming already overwhelmed people with a complex description of a problem and its solution undercuts your efforts. If they are going to disagree, you want them to disagree on the merit of your proposal, not because they don't have the energy to figure out what you are requesting.

Simplifying might mean boiling things down into three key rationales or a handful of simple options. Visual support helps. Not 10 slides, but one table that outlines your cause and effect or options with their pros and cons.

One last note: Advocacy and Inquiry

Chris Argyris, business theorist and author, first proposed the idea of balancing advocacy and inquiry in the way we approach problem-solving in organizations.

From an influence perspective, it means you need to do just as much talking about your idea (advocacy) as you do learning about the other person's perspective on your idea (inquiry).

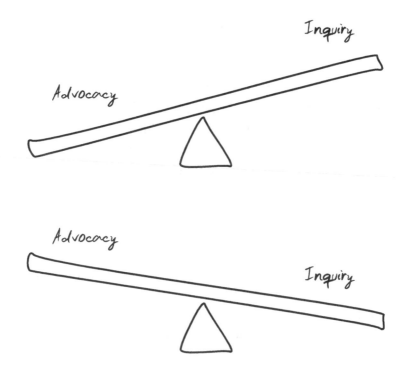

© 2019 ⃝FINERTY CONSULTING

With too much advocacy, not only do you alienate your influence target, you may not be coming up with the best solution. Too much inquiry causes you to risk coming across as wishy-washy—your target may wonder where you stand or assume you actually don't have an opinion, and your idea can get lost or overwhelmed.

Advocacy means you are describing your idea, its benefits and even its shortcomings. You are talking about other people who share your opinion or other organizations that have succeeded in implementing what you are suggesting. Inquiry involves questions to understand your partner's current state, issues, what's working and what's not, and concerns they have about your idea.

Our preparation for influence, if we do any, tends to be focused on presenting the features and benefits of our ideas. But how often do we list out the questions we want to ask? We prepare to talk, not to listen—and that is highly detrimental to influence.

> "Real answers need to be found in dialogue and interaction and, yes, our shared human condition. This means being open to one another instead of simply fighting to maintain a prescribed position."

MALCOLM BOYD

The key to a successful influence dialogue is to adopt the mindset that you only get agreement if you build an understanding of your idea, understand their perspective and rigorously work to maintain (if not improve) the partnership.

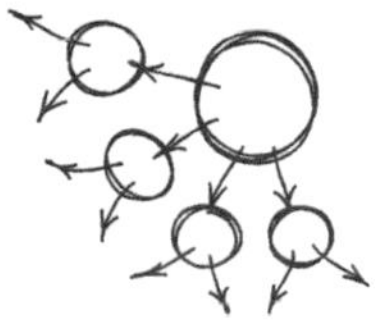

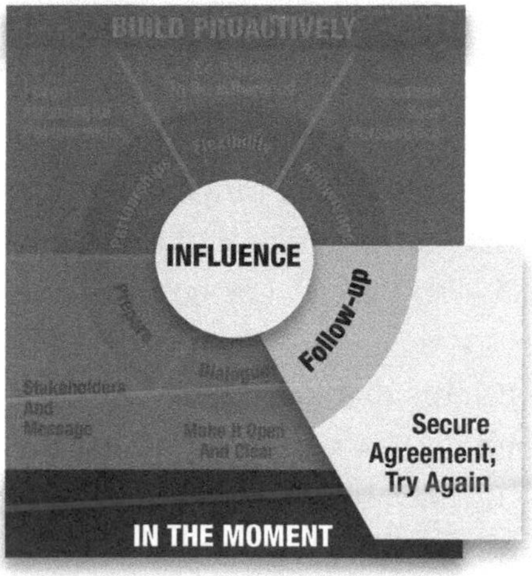

It was character that got us out of bed, commitment that moved us into action, and discipline that enabled us to follow through.

ZIG ZIGLAR

Section 6: Follow-up

Many Of Our Influence Attempts Stop At Nodding Heads; Often Much Follow-Up Is Needed To Achieve True Influence

My client Keith is probably one of the most influential people I have ever met—and you would never know it. He is laid-back, soft-spoken, eager to hear and adopt or integrate another idea. He instinctively flows through different influence tactics—he's like an influence ninja.

But what he does better than anyone I know is have the discipline to follow an idea through to completion and persevere. He knows that in order to influence, you can't stop with "nodding heads" or stop because you didn't get "nodding heads." There's a phase afterwards that differentiates between someone who gets lucky once in a while and someone who influences in a lasting, sustainable way.

This "after they commit" phase of the model wasn't included in the *Master the Matrix* book. Even I didn't see the importance of it. I essentially saw influence as a one-shot deal—you go in, get agreement or not, and then exit.

Keith doesn't see exits, he sees other doors that need to be pried and propped open to push an idea through. When he gets commitment, he follows up with people—often relentlessly, but never forcefully. He does not let that commitment fade away or stop at just words. When he gets a no, he'll take a different path or wait for the timing to be right.

Are his ideas just better than everyone else's? He would be the first to tell you they are not. But he is one of the few people I know who has that level of discipline, and it is the cornerstone of his influence in his organization.

In this section we will look at follow-up from both possible outcomes—both disagreement with your recommendation and agreement with your recommendation.

Scenario #1: Secure agreement

Great news! You've gotten agreement. But your job is not done. Have you ever had a successful influence conversation, walked out of a meeting feeling great, only to see your idea and their commitment evaporate down the line, never to be heard of again? In fast-moving organizations, this happens all the time. Why? Because people have a lot of balls in the air, and they forget. Because they nodded their head but didn't really think you were serious. They got caught up in the moment. Or they agreed, but later changed their mind. Agreements aren't solid, they need follow-up and reinforcement.

You need to make sure that what you just gained agreement on actually sticks.

© 2019 ○FINERTY CONSULTING

There are three elements of this phase:

Remind. Busy people forget. Don't let them. Immediately following the conversation, follow up in person or email, reiterating what you agreed to. Even better if that reminder is a fairly public one—so you have witnesses, so to speak.

Reinforce. Sometimes the idea is great, but the people get distracted or overwhelmed by what is needed to get it done. Make it easy for them. If you are asking for an additional resource, complete all the paperwork, so all they have to do is sign off and hit "send." If you are asking them to present information on your behalf, put all the slides together. Don't leave the conversation without dates established for a check-in. Ask them what they need from you. Make the process as streamlined and simple as possible for them. Don't let them reject an idea just because it seems like a lot of work.

Reward/Recognize. This seems basic, but make sure you thank them, even reward them with something or publicly recognize them for what they did. It's a great partnership builder and sets you up for the next time you need to influence. Let's go back to the example of a request for resources. Say you asked for an additional resource and got it. Thank the person in the short-term, but also consider six months down the line telling them the impact that this resource had on the project. This reinforces that the two of you made a great decision together and paves the way for the next time you need to tap into that person for a resource, budget or support.

Scenario #2: Try again

Not all of your recommendations will be adopted, not all your requests granted. It's how you recover that can make a huge difference. Remember the triage visual from the Prepare section?

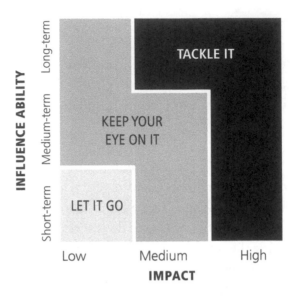

This continues to be in play if you hit a roadblock. If you are trying to influence something that has been in the "Keep Your Eye on It" category, continue to do that. Your idea will either be validated—and the timing finally right for influence, or it will become no longer necessary—it will fall into the "Let It Go" box. If your influence opportunity is in the "Tackle It" zone, and even after going through the process and getting no agreement, you think it has validity and should be tackled, you need to keep at it. What does "keep at it" look like? You have to change the people you are pulling in or the idea itself.

Here are your three options:
1. *Take it to a different stakeholder to gain momentum*
2. *Elevate or delegate*
3. *Make it more palatable*

TAKE IT TO DIFFERENT STAKEHOLDERS

When your attempt fails, think about whom you approached, brought in and eventually influenced. Were they the right people? Did you build

© 2019 ◯ FINERTY CONSULTING

enough support? Your initial attempt to influence may have been targeted to the wrong person, or you may need to do more to build an alliance. Think about casting a wider, perhaps more diverse net of stakeholders. Build alliances and approach people in different parts of the organization. They may lead you to a totally different ultimate stakeholder whom you can approach.

ELEVATE OR DELEGATE

In many complex organizations, when things get tough, we elevate up. Most organizations allow far too much of this to happen. You don't want to overplay this card—the risk is two-fold. First, you risk perceptions of dependence—not being willing or able to resolve things on your own. Second, you could be accused of over-dramatizing the situation. The more you elevate problems, the less potent elevation becomes and the more you look powerless.

When you are elevating, you are basically influencing up—you are trying to convince someone higher in the organization to be your surrogate. So how you frame your issue is critical, as is your history of elevating.

If you are going to elevate, keep these guidelines in mind:

Have the whole story. When you elevate, you need to have the full picture—not just your piece of the picture. The minute you elevate with just one side of the story, you have lost all credibility.

Don't ever cry wolf. Make sure you have done your homework and you have all the facts on the idea, points of disagreement and risk/ reward. Don't send the person you are elevating to on a wild goose chase to gain agreement that's not possible or critical to the business.

Frame it in a larger context. Describe the issue or idea in a larger context—not how it affects you, but how it affects the team and organizational goals.

Provide your ideas on steps to resolution. Do not just place the problem in their lap. Have a proposal for what to do next and all the information needed to take that next step.

You might also be able to use strong partners who view your proposal favorably as influencers over other stakeholders—"up" is not the only place to look when identifying an influence surrogate. Delegation to a partner is also a great option. Remember this visual from the Partnerships section?

| Perspective | Advocate | Ally | Surrogate |

Think about how you might pull in different people or leverage them in a different way. Could someone who is an ally actually become a surrogate in this process? Could a person who shared information behind the scenes become a more visible player?

MAKE YOUR IDEA MORE PALATABLE

Changing the "who" of your influence situation is not the only lever you can pull. You can also look at the idea itself. Is there a way you could modify the idea that would make it more palatable?

Here are a few considerations:

Make it smaller. Maybe your idea is just too overwhelming, too big to take on. Is there a way to do it on a smaller scale? Consider proposing a pilot initiative or asking stakeholders to commit only to phase one and then check in later for full or continued commitment.

© 2019 ◯FINERTY CONSULTING

Change your timeframe. Would a shorter or longer timeframe get people on board? Would a different start or end time make more sense?

Create an escape hatch. What happens if they commit, and it doesn't work? How can all those involved exit gracefully? Sometimes presenting the idea and a checkpoint to assess progress puts minds at ease. For example, if it's a resource you seek, an exit strategy might sound like, "If after six months, we aren't meeting milestones, despite the extra resource, I am willing to work to transfer the resource out and reallocate other resources."

Reframe it. Go back to Section 4. Is there a way you can reframe this? If you are framing the issue from a risk perspective, can you change your focus to the reward, or vice-versa? If you are framing it from a project milestone perspective, can you reframe to help stakeholders understand the financial risk of delay? Reframing also may lead you to rethink your stakeholders, which might just get you on the right track.

In the end, influence is more of a loop than a race to the finish line. One influence opportunity ends, and very likely it sets you up for another. Following all the way through ensures that you truly influence and builds credibility and trust—which will not soon be forgotten when the inevitable next issue needs to be resolved or decision needs to be made.

One final word

The Power Of Patience And Perseverance

Patience may be a virtue, but when working cross-functionally, *it is a necessity.* You may have days when you go home feeling like you didn't accomplish anything in all of your attempts to mold and shape those across your organization. But you did, and if you persist, you will see progress. In the words of one of my clients who struggled to gain traction in his cross-functional influence, "It's frustrating to go to work, engage in something I have a lot of passion and pride in, and yet have so few victories." I knew from talking to him that he had mastered his role more than he realized. But without patience and perseverance, he won't be able to see the progress that he is making.

I was pretty oblivious to the need for these traits well into my career.

Then I had a boss, Mary, who changed everything. Mary was kind of a Zen master. Often I would find myself in influence mode and try to force things—convince the senior leadership team to invest in a project or induce my dotted-line corporate boss to change a priority. I would run into walls over and over again and land in Mary's office frustrated and bruised. "Susan, you are planting seeds," Mary would say. "If you measure your success in days and not months or even years, you are going to go crazy in this role."

A former colleague put patience into a great perspective:

"You have just got to do what is within your control to find the issue, shine a spotlight on it, frame it, present it. What someone else chooses to do with this information is truly above your pay grade— you can't control the big picture, only your role in it. Propose what needs to change, then pin it to somebody's chest, work through it with your boss, whoever. But just keep shining a spotlight on it."

Cross-functional influence is like New York—if you can make it there, you'll make it anywhere. If you are good at what you do and engaged in the organization, you are going to see so many things that need to change, improve or go away. Don't let the purview frustrate you—appreciate it and learn to pick and choose where you will make an impact. Your influence abilities, mixed with strong partnerships, underlie every skill and every success you will have in your role.

© 2019 ◯FINERTY CONSULTING

For further reading

Ariely, D. (2008) *Predictably irrational: The hidden forces that shape our decisions.* 1st edn. New York, NY: HarperCollins Publishers.

Charan, R. (2001) *What the CEO wants you to know: The little book of big business.* United States: Crown Publishing Group.

DeLuca, J. R. (2002) *Political savvy: Systematic approaches to leadership behind-the-scenes.* 2nd edn. Berwyn, PA: Evergreen Business Group.

Finerty, S. (2015) *The Cross-Functional Influence Playbook.* United States: Two Harbors Press.

Finerty, S. Z. (2012) *Master the Matrix: 7 essentials for getting things done in complex organizations.* United States: Two Harbors Press.

McGinn, K. and Lingo, E. (no date) *Power and influence: Achieving your objectives in organizations.* Available at: https://hbr.org/product/power-and-influence-achieving-your-objectives-in-o/ an/801425-PDF-ENG

Pentland, A. (2013) *Beyond the Echo Chamber.* Available at: https://hbr.org/product/beyond-the-echo-chamber/an/R1311E-PDF-ENG

Russo, E. J. and Schoemaker, P. J. H. (1990) *Decision traps: The Ten barriers to brilliant decision-making and how to overcome them.* 1st edn. New York: Simon & Schuster.

Williams, G. A. and Miller, R. B. (2002) *Change the way you persuade.* Available at: https://hbr.org/2002/05/change-the-way-you-persuade/ar/1